CAMBRIDGE
UNIVERSITY PRESS

Cambridge Global English

LEARNER'S BOOK 7

Chris Barker & Libby Mitchell

Contents

Contents

Use of English	Cross-curricular links	Vocabulary	21st-century skills
-ing forms Remember: present simple and present continuous Remember: superlatives Expressing the future (present continuous, *going to*, *will/shall*, present simple)	Health education Geography	Outdoor equipment and activities, including adventure sports	Learning to learn: Learn words in groups to help remember them Critical thinking: Give reasons in a discussion about the role of nature in health and well-being; put documents in a logical order, according to chronological sequence Creative thinking: Write a scene for a story, using direct speech and descriptive language Collaborative working: Pair work, group work, projects
Compound nouns Abstract nouns Pronouns *everyone*, *anyone*, *no one*; *everything*, *anything*, *nothing* Comparative adverbs	Physical education	Sports and sports equipment Football	Learning to learn: Learn vocabulary by playing a definitions game; use reference resources to find information Social responsibility: Discuss the role of international sport in changing attitudes and opinions Critical thinking: Discuss the issue of using animals in sport; summarise points of view Collaborative working: Pair work, group work, projects
adjective + preposition, adjective + infinitive verb + *-ing* verb + infinitive, verb + object + infinitive	Science and technology Citizenship	Jobs Adjectives to describe personality	Learning to learn: Use clues to predict what you're going to hear in a listening exercise Social responsibility: Discuss what makes a good role model Critical thinking: Discuss how science and technology can make a difference to people's lives Creative thinking: Write a scene for a film based on a narrative extract Collaborative working: Pair work, group work, projects
Remember: present perfect for events in the recent past Connectives: *because*, *so that*, *as*, *therefore*, *however*, *although* Quantifiers: *both (of)*, *each other/one another*, *either of/neither of* Complex nouns phrases Past continuous	Media studies Maths	Journalism Expressions connected with social media	Critical thinking: Summarise opinions of people discussing a news report; differentiate between real and fake news; identify implied meaning; evaluate the advantages and disadvantages of social media Collaborative working: Pair work, group work, projects
Remember: reported statements Reported questions and requests Indefinite and quantifying pronouns Multi-word verbs *if* and *unless* clauses, zero and first conditional	Science and technology	Digital technology	Learning to learn: Learn expressions to make your writing and conversation sound more natural Social responsibility: Discuss the advantages and disadvantages of robots and of technology in farming Creative thinking: Write a factual description based on a model Collaborative working: Pair work, group work, projects

How to use this book

In this book you will find lots of different features to help your learning.

The Remember section at the start of the book contains questions and notes to help you remember some key grammar points.

What you will learn in the unit or lesson.

In this lesson you will…

- **talk** and **write** about meeting and greeting in your culture
- **read** and **understand** a text about famous gifts in history
- **ask for** and **give** ideas and opinions

Big questions to find out what you know already.

Getting started

"Who are the most important people in your life?"

Important words and their meanings. These words are included on wordlists in the Teacher's Resource.

Hello	How are things?	Good morning	Goodbye!	See you later	Hi
Bye	Nice to meet you	See you	How are you?	Good afternoon	Hey

The key words feature includes vocabulary from other subjects.

Key words: History

army
independence
soldier
war

Read real texts with helpful glossaries.

[0] hullabaloo: a lot of excitement and noise surrounding an event
[0] orchard: a place where fruit trees are grown
[1] snorted: made a loud noise by forcing air out through the nose, like a horse
[2] steadily: slowly and gradually
[14] urged: strongly advised
[15] twitched: made a sudden short nervous movement

Use of English boxes and accompanying questions present the main grammar points in a unit.

Use of English **Past simple: regular and irregular**

The past tense forms of these verbs are in the text. Find them.
regular: sail, ***sailed*** pull wait remain
irregular: be, ***was*** have build leave think become
Questions in the past simple:
*Two nations were at war. **Who were** they?*
***What did** the Greeks **build**?*
***Did** all the Greeks **sail** away from Troy?*
Negatives in the past simple:
*The Trojans **didn't know** that there were Greek soldiers inside the horse.*
*The horse **wasn't** a real horse and it **wasn't** a real gift.*

A brief revision of other language points.

Remember

You can use *should* and *shouldn't* to ask for and give advice.
*What **should** you take when you visit friends and family?*
***Should** you be careful when giving flowers?*
*You **should** wrap your gifts.*
*You **shouldn't** give white flowers.*

Strategies you can use to help you with your learning.

Language tip

Use the pronoun 'you' to mean 'people in general'.
In China, you bow when you meet someone.

Questions to help you think about how you learn.

- Was it useful to write an account of the family member before you answered the questions? Why?
- Did anybody ask you a question you couldn't answer? What did you say?

Questions that cover what you have learned in each unit. If you can answer these, you are ready to move on to the next unit.

Check your progress

General knowledge quiz

1 What did the Greeks leave for the Trojans at the gates of their city, Troy? Why did they leave it there?

2 Look at the photo. What is it?

This is what you have learned in the unit.

Summary checklist

- [ ] I know about some customs of meeting and greeting and I can talk about them.
- [ ] I know about some famous gifts in history.
- [ ] I can have a conversation about giving gifts.
- [ ] I can describe my family members and my family history.
- [ ] I know about tracing ancestors.
- [ ] I can talk about my experiences at secondary school.
- [ ] I can have a conversation about giving gifts.

Audio is available with the Digital Learner's Book, Teacher's Resource or Digital Classroom.

Video is available with Digital Classroom.

Lessons 1 and 4: The **Think about it** lessons introduce topic vocabulary

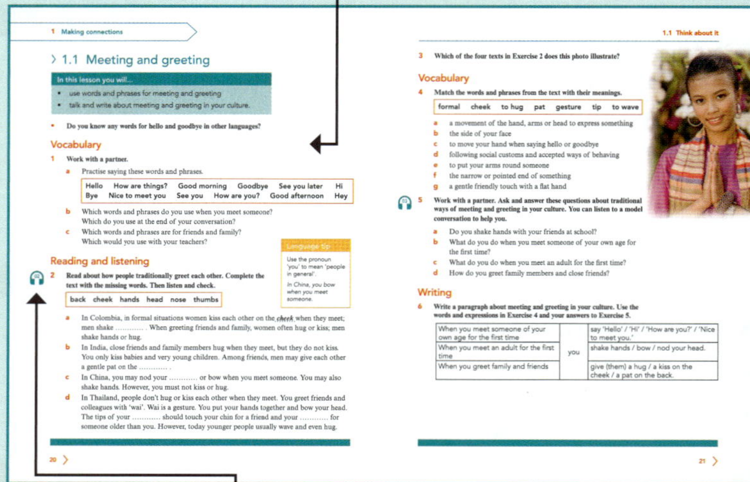

Engage with the topic of the unit and generate discussion using the image, the video and the big question.

These lessons include listening activities.

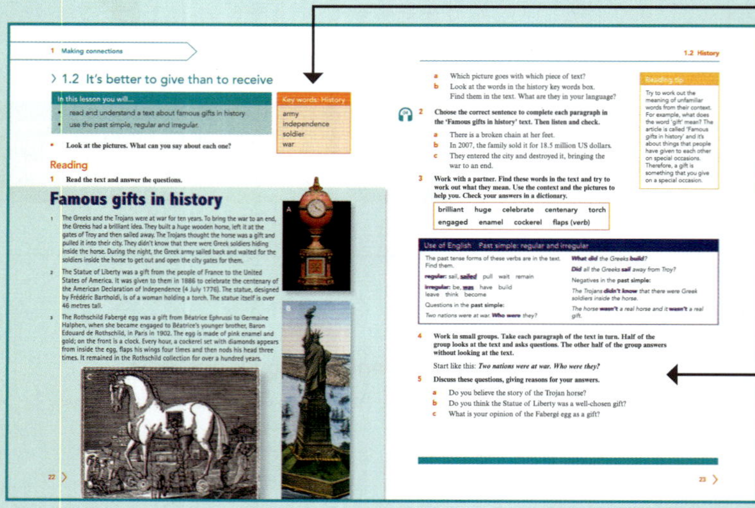

Lessons 2 and 5: The **cross-curricular** lessons prepare learners to learn in English across the curriculum.

In this lesson you'll find Key words boxes.

A key text exposes learners to cross-curricular language.

There are opportunities to think critically about the information in the text.

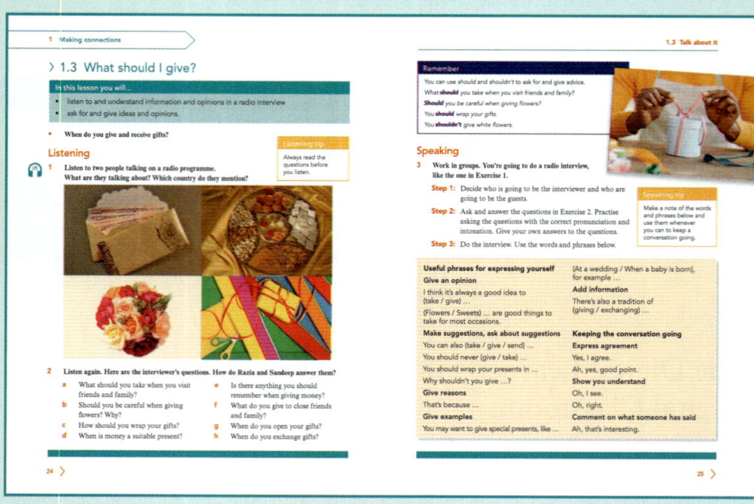

Lessons 3 and 6: The **Talk about it** lessons develop learners' speaking skills.

Listen to models and practise pronunciation and intonation.

Listening models and speaking tips provide scaffolding for speaking.

Lesson 7:
The **Write about it** section supports learners in writing a variety of text types.

Step-by-step tasks supports learners in their planning, writing and editing.

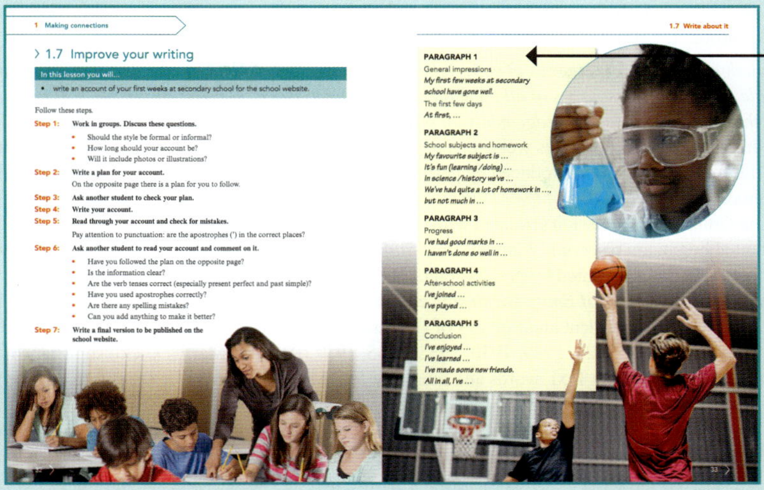

Model texts with call-outs support the writing process.

Assessment ideas and sample learner answers can be found in the Teacher's Resource.

Lesson 8:
The **Project challenge** lesson provides a choice of projects. and provides an opportunity to consolidate learning from the unit

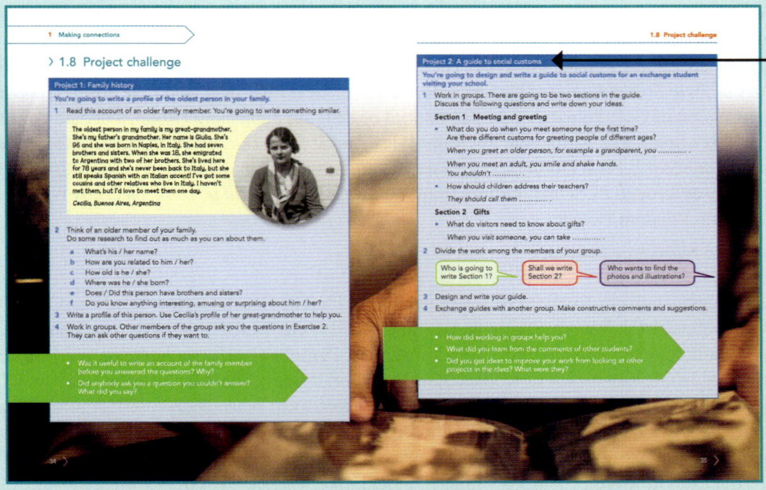

Projects encourage 21st-century skills such as research, collaboration, and creativity.

Self-and peer-evaluation checklists for projects are available in the Teacher's Resource.

Lesson 9:
The **Read and respond** lesson is based on authentic texts and includes fiction, non-fiction, poetry and autobiography.

The audio can be played the first time you meet the story, before learners read the text.

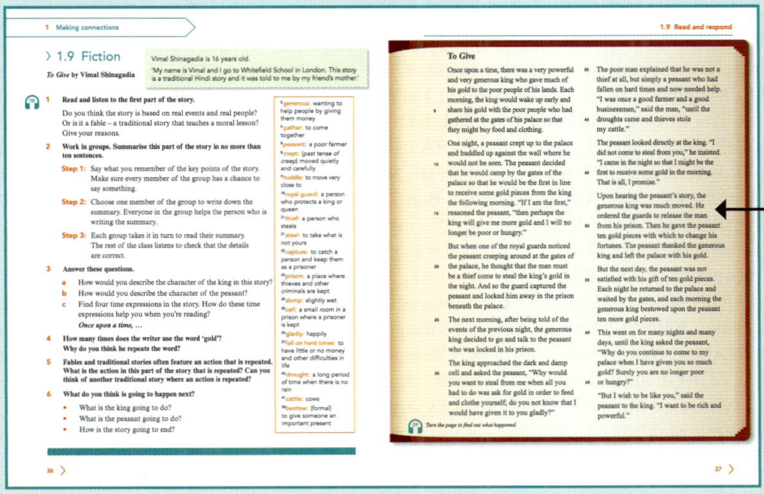

The literature is used as a platform for work on values.

There is also an opportunity for creative writing.

Acknowledgements

The authors and publishers would like to thank the following for reviewing Stage 7: Nina Ambarwati, Insan Cendekia Madani School; F. Rizwana R. Azhar, Lyceum International School; Sarah Farook, Lyceum International School.

The authors and publishers acknowledge the following sources of copyright material and are grateful for the permissions granted. While every effort has been made, it has not always been possible to identify the sources of all the material used, or to trace all copyright holders. If any omissions are brought to our notice, we will be happy to include the appropriate acknowledgements on reprinting.

Unit 1: 'To Give' by Vimal Shingadia, from the World Stories website, a collection of stories by children collected by Kids Out; **Unit 2:** 'Tuen Ng' (The Dragon Boat Races) by Judith Nicholls © Judith Nicholls 2020, reproduced by permission of the author; 'Chinese New Year' by John Foster. Reproduced by permission of the author; **Unit 3:** 'Ode to my Shoes' from *Bellybutton of the Moon* by Francisco X. Alarcon. Text Copyright ©1998 by Francisco X. Alarcon. Illustrations Copyright © 1998 by Maria Christina Gonzalez. Permission arranged with Children's Book Press, an imprint of Lee & Low Books, Inc., New York, NY 10016. All rights not specifically granted herein are reserved; 'Flannel' from *Toasting Marshmallows: Camping Poems* by Kristine O'Connell George. Text copyright © 2001 by Kristine O'Connell George. Reprinted by permission of Houghton Mifflin Harcourt Publishing Company and Kristine O'Connell George. All rights reserved; 'A Slash of Blue' from *The Poems of Emily Dickinson*, edited by Thomas H. Johnson, Cambridge, Mass.: The Belknap Press of Harvard University Press, Copyright © 1951, 1955 by the President and Fellows of Harvard College. Copyright © renewed 1979, 1983 by the President and Fellows of Harvard College. Copyright © 1914, 1918, 1919, 1924, 1929, 1930, 1932, 1935, 1937, 1942, by Martha Dickinson Bianchi. Copyright © 1952, 1957, 1958, 1963, 1965, by Mary L. Hampson; **Unit 4;** 'Big Yellow Taxi' words and music by Joni Mitchell, Copyright © 1970 (Renewed) Crazy Crow Music, All Rights (Excluding Print) Administered by Sony/ATV Tunes LLC, Exclusive Print Rights Administered by Alfred Music, All Rights Reserved Used By Permission of Alfred Music; 'My City Was Gone' by Chrissie Hynde © Copyright 1982 BMG Rights Management (UK) Limited, a BMG Company. All Rights Reserved. International Copyright Secured. Used by Permission of Hal Leonard Europe Limited; **Unit 5:** Excerpt(s) from Forest Bathing: *How Trees Can Help You Find Health and Happiness* by Dr. Qing Li, copyright © 2018 by Qing Li. Used by permission of Viking Books, an imprint of Penguin Publishing Group, a division of Penguin Random House LLC. All rights reserved; Excerpt from Hullabaloo in the Guava Orchard by Kiran Desai, copyright © 1998 by Kiran Desai, used by the permission of Faber & Faber and Grove/Atlantic, Inc. Any third party use of this material, outside of this publication, is prohibited; **Unit 6:** Excerpt from Bend it Like Beckham by Narinder Dhami, reproduced by permission of Hodder Children's Books, an imprint of Hachette Children's Books, and United Agents; **Unit 7:** Interview with Hannah Herbst from Wharton High School website; Excerpt(s) from *The Boy Who Harnessed The Wind: Young Readers Edition* by William Kamkwamba and Bryan Mealer, text copyright © 2015 by William Kamkwamba and Bryan Mealer. Used by permission of Dial Books for Young Readers, an imprint of Penguin Young Readers Group, a division of Penguin Random House LLC. All rights reserved; **Unit 8:** 'Australia to impose 24-hour curfew on all cats to protect endangered species' by Siobhan Fenton in The Independent, July 2015 © Siobhan Fenton/The Independent; Excerpt(s) from *Separated @ Birth: A True Love Story of Twin Sisters Reunited* by Anais Bordier, Samantha Futerman, and Lisa Pulitzer, copyright © 2014 by Anais Bordier and Samantha Futerman. Used by permission of G. P. Putnam's Sons, an imprint of Penguin Publishing Group, a division of Penguin Random House LLC. All rights reserved; **Unit 9:** 'Inside Bengaluru's first Robot Restaurant' by Ralph Alex Arakal *from The Indian Express;* 'Meet these robot waiters giving a futuristic spin to dining' by Tenzin Norzom from *Your Story;* Ernst Gombrich, A Little History of the World, Illustrated Edition, 2011 edition, Yale University Press, Reproduced with permission of the Licensor through PLSclear; Extract from *A History of the World in 100 Objects* by Neil MacGregor published by Allen Lane, 2010, used by permission of Penguin Random House.

Thanks to the following for permission to reproduce images:

Cover image: manoa/Getty Images

Remember: SDI Productions/GI; Benedetta Barbanti/EyeEm/GI; Jose Luis Pelaez Inc/GI; Courtney Hale/GI; Nora Carol Photography/GI; Nitat Termmee/GI; Westend61/GI **Unit 1:** revetina01/GI; Wavebreakmedia/GI; ranplett/GI; Peter Macdiarmid/GI; Ann Ronan Pictures/Print Collector/G; Universal History Archive/GI; JOAT/Shutterstock; Uniquely india/GI; Dianazh/GI; Pogrebkov/GI; mediaphotos/GI; Hero Images/GI; Grant Faint/GI; PeopleImages/GI; Kali9/GI; MachineHeadz/GI; Rawpixel/GI; lcodacci/GI; BraunS/GI; Chronicle/Alamy; Irina Marwan/GI; **Unit 2:** Westend61/GI; Jethuyng/GI; ferrantraite/GI; Dinodia Photo/GI; Hemant Mehta/GI; highviews/Shutterstock; Nhac Nguyen/GI; Andrey Nikitin/GI; Universal History Archive/GI; Colombia Landmarks and People by Vision/Alamy Stock Photo; Jake Jung/GI; Afriandi/GI; Jeremy Woodhouse/GI; Ariel Skelley/GI; tbc; Tao Zhang/GI; Ferrantraite/GI; Belchonock/GI; arnau2098/GI; muratart/Shutterstock; Nanut Bovorn/GI; Karn Bulsuk/GI; YuenWu/GI; VCG/GI; Visual China Group via GI; **Unit 3:** Daniel Limpi/EyeEm/GI; Monkey Business Images/Stockbroker/GI; ZU_09/GI; Art Media/Print Collector/GI; Universal History Archive/GI; Image taken from Wikimedia; ViewStock/GI; Backiris/GI; Wabeno/GI; Andresr/GI; Andresr/GI; Jasmin Merdan/GI; GCShutter/GI; Image by Ecoalf; dpa picture alliance/Alamy Stock Photo; Image from UNICEF used with the permission; Barry Winiker/GI; Manfred Gottschalk/GI; iStock/GI; AFP/Stringer/GI; Kwanchai_Khammuean/GI; Joseph Pierce/GI; Nora Carol Photography/GI; Wendy Maeda/The Boston Globe/GI; Swisshippo/GI; **Unit 4:** Smartshots International/GI; Marcio Jose Bastos Silva/Shutterstock; Coward_lion/GI; Scaliger/GI; Sylvain Grandadam/Gamma-Rapho/GI; Trainman111/GI; Eric Cabanis/GI; Science & Society Picture Library/SSPL/GI; Oxford Science Archive/Print Collector/GI; The Print Collector/GI; Image Source/GI; Anass Bachar/GI; Agustavop/GI; Walter Bibikow/GI; ferrantraite/GI; Martín Jaggi/EyeEm/GI; tunart/GI; Education Images/Universal Images Group/GI; Marco Bottigelli/GI George Pachantouris/GI; Tumjang/GI; Henryk Sadura/GI; Miemo Penttinen-miemo.net/GI; GAB Archive/Redferns/GI; Tetra images RF/GI; Blaine Harrington III/GI; J.C. Marciniak/GI; ZU_09/GI; **Unit 5:** YinYang/GI; Yellow Dog Productions/GI; RunPhoto/GI; Yellow Dog/GI; Extreme-Photographer/GI; Rafael Ben-Ari/GI; Tim Clayton/Corbis/GI; traumlichtfabrik/GI; Sol de Zuasnabar Brebbia/GI; East Road/Ascent Xmedia/GI; Ishan Tankha/The The India Today Group/GI; amanalang/GI; Artur Lebedev/TASS/GI; iStockphoto/GI; Science Photo Library RF/GI; Oleksiy Maksymenko/GI; Berkah/GI; **Unit 6:** Glyn Kirk/GI; FatCamera/GI; Darrell Hoemann/GI; Mike Powell/GI; Saeed Khan/GI; sergio_kumer/GI; Jana Leon/GI; Hindustan Times/GI; Martin Rose/GI; Justin Setterfield/Stringer/GI; angelhell/GI; Bob Thomas Sports Photography/GI; Tim Clayton-Corbis/GI; Max Paddler/GI; miteman/GI; Francois Nel/GI (x2); Karim Sahib/GI; Friedemann Vogel/Stringer/GI; Buda Mendes/GI; Rivers Dale/GI; Amin Mohammad Jamali/GI; Look and Learn/Bridgeman; benoit/GI; Tottenham Hotspur FC/GI; Christopher Furlong/GI; **Unit 7:** Dougal Waters/GI; Tom Werner/GI; Mike Harrington/GI; aydinmutlu/GI; Morsa Images/GI;Rawpixel/GI; Alan Diaz/AP/Shutterstock; 35007/GI; photo supplied by Alex Knoll, used with kind permission; kali9/GI (x2); Dan Kitwood/GI; Watcharin Panyawutso/EyeEm/GI; Morsa Images/GI; Melodious Vision/GI; Klaus Vedfelt/GI; EyeEm/GI; Fabrice Coffrini/GI; Lifestyle pictures/Alamy Stock Photo; Kali9/GI; **Unit 8:** Prangkul Ruangsri/GI; Hill Street Studios/GI; SolStock/GI; Heritage Images/GI; Fine Art Images/Heritage Images/GI; Interfoto/Alamy Stock Photo; Fox Photos/Stringer/GI; marieclaudelemay/GI;sorbetto/GI; Dustin Finkelstein/GI; Maskot/GI; yulkapopkova/GI; Jean-philippe WALLET/GI; amanalang/GI; fotostorm/GI; SolStock/GI; Dustin Finkelstein/GI; **Unit 9:** MarsYu/GI; everythingpossible/GI; Manjunath Kiran/GI; T2 Images/GI; Guido Mieth/GI; Busakorn Pongparnit/GI; Jasmin Merdan/GI; Nacho Calonge/GI; Image taken from https://www.designboom.com; Cavan Images/GI; Amir Mukhtar/GI; Tetra Images/GI; Ron Watts/GI; alexandercreative/GI; Sharon Lapkin/GI; Heritage Images/GI; sergeichekman/GI;

Key: GI= Getty Images

Remember

You can use the following notes and exercises to help you remember some key grammar points.

Verbs

Words like *do, go, have, live* and *be* are **verbs**. We change the form of the verb to show the time we are referring to.

Present

We use the **present simple** to talk about:

- things that are true now *I live in the city centre.*
- things that are always true *Water boils at 100 °C.*
- things that happen regularly. *I play football every Saturday.*

+	–	?
I live in the city centre.	I don't live in a village.	Do you live in a city?
He / She lives in the city centre.	He / She doesn't live in a village.	Does he / she live in a city?

We use the **present continuous** to talk about:

- things that are happening at the time we are speaking *I'm doing my homework.*
- temporary situations. *I'm staying with my grandparents at the moment.*

+	–	?
I'm doing my homework.	I'm not watching TV.	Are you watching TV?

1 **Choose present simple or present continuous to complete these sentences.**

a My parents are both doctors. They ***work*** (*work*) at the local hospital.
b Sorry, I can't talk now. I .... (*have*) dinner.
c Sshh! Be quiet! We .... (*watch*) a really good film.
d You can borrow my laptop. I .... (*not use*) it at the moment.
e He's vegetarian so he .... (*not eat*) hamburgers.

Past

We use the **past simple** to talk about things that happened at a particular time in the past.

+	–	?
I went to the cinema yesterday.	*I didn't go to the match.*	*Did you go to the match?*

To form the past simple of some verbs, you add **-ed** or **-d** to the infinitive (*walk* → *walked, like* → *liked*). Other past simple forms are irregular. There is a list of them on page 18.

We use the **past continuous** to talk about things that were in progress at a time in the past, often when something else happened: *I was cycling to school when it started to rain.*

+	–	?
I was cycling to school.	*I wasn't walking to school.*	*Were you cycling to school?*

2 Put the verbs in the correct tense: past simple or past continuous.

- **a** ***We saw*** (*We / see*) Niagara Falls when ***we were flying*** (*we / fly*) over Canada.
- **b** .... (*I / look*) at my phone when .... (*I / walk*) into a police officer.
- **c** .... (*You / not / hear*) what I said because .... (*you / not / listen*).
- **d** Sorry, ... (*I / do*) my homework when .... (*you / call*), so I didn't answer.
- **e** .... (*My sister / not / go*) to the family party because .... (*she / travel*) for work.

We use the **present perfect simple** when we want to talk about past actions that are connected to the present time.

+	–	?
I've made a cake.	*I haven't made any biscuits.*	*Have you made anything?*

To make the present perfect, you need the past participle (*made*, in the sentence *I've made a cake*). There is a list of irregular past participles on page 18.

There is an important difference between the past participles *gone* and *been*:

She's gone to the beach. (She is on her way to the beach *or* She is at the beach now.)

She's been to the beach. (She is now back home again.)

3 **Use the present perfect simple to complete these sentences.**

a ***I've just had*** (*I / just / have*) some good news. I've got a place at the summer music school!

b I think ………… (*you / take*) enough photos, Samir. Put your camera away, please!

c ………… (*I / not / see*) you for ages. Where have you been?

d ………… (*We / not / see*) the new sports centre. What's it like?

e I couldn't eat anything, thank you. ………… (*I / already / have*) two ice creams!

Future

We can talk about the **future** in English by using:

• *will* (for predictions or decisions at the time of speaking)	*I will (I'll) see you later.*
• *going to* (for decisions you have already made)	*I'm going to have riding lessons in the holidays.*
• the present simple (for timetables, fixed times and dates)	*The next lesson starts at 10 o'clock.*
• the present continuous (for fixed plans, with a time and/or place).	*We're having a barbecue on Saturday. Come if you can!*

4 **Choose the best option.**

a I'm sure she ***will get*** / *is getting* very good grades in her exams next term.

b I *'m staying* / *will stay* at home this evening. Do you want to come and watch a film?

c When I'm older, I *'m going to build* / *am building* my own house.

d You can't go out on Saturday. Your aunt and uncle *will come* / *are coming* to visit!

e The school holidays *are going to begin* / *begin* on 11 July.

Passive

We use the passive when we want to focus on what happens or what happened, not on a person. We can use:

• the present passive	*Tea is grown in China and India.*
• the past passive.	*The Suez Canal was opened in 1869.*

5 **Make these sentences passive. Be careful: you need to decide whether to use the present passive or the past passive.**

- **a** We serve breakfast from 8 until 10. ***Breakfast is served from 8 until 10.***
- **b** Someone called you today at 19.30. ***You were called today at 19.30.***
- **c** They teach Spanish at my school.
- **d** We take exams in May and June.
- **e** Someone recognised him.

Verb short forms

We use short forms in English, particularly in conversation and in informal writing.

am →	'm	*I'm from Indonesia.*	are →	're	*They're good at maths.*
is →	's	*He's South African.*	would →	'd	*We'd like to see that film.*
has →	's	*She's got a twin sister.*	will →	'll	*We'll call you later.*
have →	've	*We've been to Singapore.*			

To make negative short forms:

- use *not* after *I'm* *I'm not …*
- shorten *not* to *n't*

is not → isn't	were not → weren't	had not → hadn't	did not → didn't
are not → aren't	has not → hasn't	do not → don't	
was not → wasn't	have not → haven't	does not → doesn't	

- add *n't* to modals

must not → mustn't should not → shouldn't need not → needn't

But note:

can + not → cannot or can't will + not → won't shall + not → shan't

6 **Test yourself. Cover the short forms and try to write them from memory.**

Modals (*can, should,* etc.) and similar verbs

can / could / be able to	may / might		
must	have to / have got to	should / ought to	needn't
will / would			

You can add the verbs to other verbs to express ideas such as:

- what is possible or not possible — *I can't play football today, but I could play tomorrow.*
- what is allowed or not — *You mustn't run in the corridors.*
- what is necessary or not — *We don't have to go to school on Saturdays.*
- what is probable or not — *It might rain tomorrow.*
- what is the right thing to do. — *You should listen when your teacher is talking.*

Can, could, may, might, must, should, needn't, will and *would* don't change.
They are the same for all persons.

I / You / He / She / We / You / They should read this book. It's very good.

You can use *can, may* and *could*:

- to ask permission — *Can / May we go now?*
- to ask politely — *Could you repeat that, please?*

7 Rewrite these sentences so that they have a similar meaning, using the verb in green.

a Would it be possible for me to borrow your pen? **could**
Could I borrow your pen?

b I think it would be a very good idea for you to visit your grandmother next weekend. **should**

c Do you want me to help you? **can**

d It's very important that you are on time for your appointment. **mustn't**

e I'm sorry, I really can't stay any longer. **have to**

Multi-word verbs

Multi-word verbs are compound verbs made up of a verb and another word or other words.

- verb + preposition — *get into, look for, put on*
- verb + adverb — *get up, find out, look up*
- verb + adverb + preposition — *get away with, get on with, look forward to*

Sometimes the meaning of the multi-word verb is close to the meaning of the words in it:

We ***stand up*** *when a teacher comes into our class.*

Sometimes the meaning is quite different from the meaning of each word:

I'm ***looking after*** *my neighbours' goldfish while they're on holiday.*

8 Choose from the words in the box to complete these sentences.

in	on	out	up

a What time do you get .... in the morning on a school day?

b Come ...., hurry up! We're late!

c I'll text you when I find .... what time the game starts.

d I've known her since we were at primary school. We've always got .... well.

e I don't know what 'mystery' means, but we can look it .... in a dictionary.

f I have to make a phone call. Please carry .... with your work.

g Sorry, I can't come out this evening. I have to stay .... to look after my brother.

h It's getting cold. Put your coat .... if you're going out.

i Your train gets .... at 4.30, so I'll be there to meet you at the station.

j It's getting dark. Could you turn the light ...., please?

Punctuation

9 Work in pairs. Read the punctuation guide and discuss it with your partner. Is there anything in it that is new to you?

Punctuation guide

Use capital letters for:

- the beginning of a sentence — *A sentence starts with a capital letter.*
- days of the week and months of the year — *Monday, Tuesday, January, February*
- public holidays, places, events — *New Year's Day, the North Pole, the Olympic Games*
- languages — *English, Spanish, Mandarin*
- countries and nationalities — *China, Chinese*

Use a full stop [.]

- at the end of a sentence — *A sentence ends with a full stop.*
- in decimals — *0.25 (zero point two five)*
- but not with letters for well-known titles. — *UN, USA, UAE*

Use a comma [,]

- in lists of things (but not before *and*)
  We need beans, rice, tomatoes and pasta.
- to separate direct speech from reporting verbs
  'My name's Inaya,' she said.
  (say, answer, etc.)
- when you add extra information in a sentence
  My grandfather, who grew up in India, cooks the best curries in the world!
- between adjectives before a noun
  It's a useful, well-written, informative book.
- but commas are not always needed between short adjectives.
  It was a warm sunny day.

Use a colon [:]

- to introduce a list.
  For the exam you will need the following: a pencil, a ruler, an eraser and a calculator.

Use a semi-colon [;]

- after a colon in a list that contains longer phrases
  Remember the following: write your name at the top of the page; read the questions carefully and plan your answers.
- to join closely connected ideas, which could be separate sentences, in one sentence.
  Amaya is very good at science; she wants to be a doctor.

Use a question mark [?]

- after direct questions
  Do you like watching football on TV, Eric?
- but not after indirect questions.
  I asked Eric if he liked watching football on TV.

Use an exclamation mark [!]

- at the end of sentences that express amusement, annoyance, fear, surprise, etc.
  That is absolutely ridiculous!
- after commands
  Don't sit on the desk!
- after words or sounds that express strong feelings
  Wow! Amazing!

Use inverted commas [' ' or " "]

- to show direct speech.
  'If you don't listen, you won't learn,' she said.

Use an apostrophe [']

- in possessive forms
  The students' presentations were really good.
- in verb short forms.
  I'm pleased. You've worked hard.

Common irregular verbs

10 Work with a partner. Test yourselves.

Student A: Cover the past simple forms in the first group (*be* to *keep*).
Say the infinitive and ask Student B to give you the past simple.

Student B: Cover the past simple forms in the second group (*know* to *write*). Say the infinitive and ask Student A to give you the past simple.

Do the same for the past participles.

Infinitive	Past simple	Past participle
be	was / were	been
become	became	become
begin	began	begun
bite	bit	bitten
break	broke	broken
bring	brought	brought
build	built	built
buy	bought	bought
catch	caught	caught
choose	chose	chosen
come	came	come
cost	cost	cost
cut	cut	cut
do	did	done
draw	drew	drawn
drink	drank	drunk
drive	drove	driven
eat	ate	eaten
fall	fell	fallen
feel	felt	felt
fight	fought	fought
find	found	found
fly	flew	flown
forget	forgot	forgotten
get	got	got
give	gave	given
go	went	gone / been
grow	grew	grown
have	had	had
hear	heard	heard
hit	hit	hit
hold	held	held
hurt	hurt	hurt
keep	kept	kept

Infinitive	Past simple	Past participle
know	knew	known
leave	left	left
lend	lent	lent
lose	lost	lost
make	made	made
meet	met	met
pay	paid	paid
put	put	put
read	read	read
ride	rode	ridden
run	ran	run
say	said	said
see	saw	seen
sell	sold	sold
send	sent	sent
shut	shut	shut
sing	sang	sung
sit	sat	sat
sleep	slept	slept
speak	spoke	spoken
spend	spent	spent
stand	stood	stood
steal	stole	stolen
swim	swam	swum
take	took	taken
teach	taught	taught
tell	told	told
think	thought	thought
throw	threw	thrown
understand	understood	understood
wake (up)	woke (up)	woken (up)
wear	wore	worn
win	won	won
write	wrote	written

1 Making connections

In this unit you will...

- **talk** and **write** about meeting and greeting in your culture
- **read** and **understand** a text about famous gifts in history
- **ask for** and **give** ideas and opinions
- **listen** to a description of a family and write about your own family
- **read** about people tracing their ancestors
- **listen** to students talking about what they've done at school
- **write** an account of your first weeks at secondary school for the school website.

Getting started

" Who are the most important people in your life? "

Watch this!

1.1 Meeting and greeting

In this lesson you will...

- use words and phrases for meeting and greeting
- talk and write about meeting and greeting in your culture.

- **Do you know any words for hello and goodbye in other languages?**

Vocabulary

1 **Work with a partner.**

a Practise saying these words and phrases.

Hello	How are things?	Good morning	Goodbye	See you later	Hi
Bye	Nice to meet you	See you	How are you?	Good afternoon	Hey

b Which words and phrases do you use when you meet someone? Which do you use at the end of your conversation?

c Which words and phrases are for friends and family? Which would you use with your teachers?

Language tip

Use the pronoun 'you' to mean 'people in general'.

In China, you bow when you meet someone.

Reading and listening

02 2 **Read about how people traditionally greet each other. Complete the text with the missing words. Then listen and check.**

back	cheek	hands	head	nose	thumbs

a In Colombia, in formal situations women kiss each other on the *cheek* when they meet; men shake ………… . When greeting friends and family, women often hug or kiss; men shake hands or hug.

b In India, close friends and family members hug when they meet, but they do not kiss. You only kiss babies and very young children. Among friends, men may give each other a gentle pat on the ………… .

c In China, you may nod your ………… or bow when you meet someone. You may also shake hands. However, you must not kiss or hug.

d In Thailand, people don't hug or kiss each other when they meet. You greet friends and colleagues with 'wai'. Wai is a gesture. You put your hands together and bow your head. The tips of your ………… should touch your chin for a friend and your ………… for someone older than you. However, today younger people usually wave and even hug.

3 **Which of the four texts in Exercise 2 does this photo illustrate?**

Vocabulary

4 **Match the words and phrases from the text with their meanings.**

formal	cheek	to hug	pat	gesture	tip	to wave

a a movement of the hand, arms or head to express something
b the side of your face
c to move your hand when saying hello or goodbye
d following social customs and accepted ways of behaving
e to put your arms round someone
f the narrow or pointed end of something
g a gentle friendly touch with a flat hand

03

5 **Work with a partner. Ask and answer these questions about traditional ways of meeting and greeting in your culture. You can listen to a model conversation to help you.**

a Do you shake hands with your friends at school?
b What do you do when you meet someone of your own age for the first time?
c What do you do when you meet an adult for the first time?
d How do you greet family members and close friends?

Writing

6 **Write a paragraph about meeting and greeting in your culture. Use the words and expressions in Exercise 4 and your answers to Exercise 5.**

When you meet someone of your own age for the first time	you	say 'Hello' / 'Hi' / 'How are you?' / 'Nice to meet you.'
When you meet an adult for the first time		shake hands / bow / nod your head.
When you greet family and friends		give (them) a hug / a kiss on the cheek / a pat on the back.

1.2 It's better to give than to receive

In this lesson you will...

- read and understand a text about famous gifts in history
- use the past simple, regular and irregular.

Key words: History

army
independence
soldier
war

- **Look at the pictures. What can you say about each one?**

Reading

1 **Read the text and answer the questions.**

Famous gifts in history

1 The Greeks and the Trojans were at war for ten years. To bring the war to an end, the Greeks had a brilliant idea. They built a huge wooden horse, left it at the gates of Troy and then sailed away. The Trojans thought the horse was a gift and pulled it into their city. They didn't know that there were Greek soldiers hiding inside the horse. During the night, the Greek army sailed back and waited for the soldiers inside the horse to get out and open the city gates for them.

2 The Statue of Liberty was a gift from the people of France to the United States of America. It was given to them in 1886 to celebrate the centenary of the American Declaration of Independence (4 July 1776). The statue, designed by Frédéric Bartholdi, is of a woman holding a torch. The statue itself is over 46 metres tall.

3 The Rothschild Fabergé egg was a gift from Béatrice Ephrussi to Germaine Halphen, when she became engaged to Béatrice's younger brother, Baron Edouard de Rothschild, in Paris in 1902. The egg is made of pink enamel and gold; on the front is a clock. Every hour, a cockerel set with diamonds appears from inside the egg, flaps his wings four times and then nods his head three times. It remained in the Rothschild collection for over a hundred years.

a Which picture goes with which piece of text?

b Look at the words in the history key words box. Find them in the text. What are they in your language?

04

2 Choose the correct sentence to complete each paragraph in the 'Famous gifts in history' text. Then listen and check.

a There is a broken chain at her feet.

b In 2007, the family sold it for 18.5 million US dollars.

c They entered the city and destroyed it, bringing the war to an end.

3 Work with a partner. Find these words in the text and try to work out what they mean. Use the context and the pictures to help you. Check your answers in a dictionary.

brilliant	huge	celebrate	centenary	torch
engaged	enamel	cockerel	flaps (*verb*)	

Reading tip

Try to work out the meaning of unfamiliar words from their context. For example, what does the word 'gift' mean? The article is called 'Famous *gifts* in history' and it's about things that people have *given* to each other on special occasions. Therefore, a gift is something that you give on a special occasion.

Use of English Past simple: regular and irregular

The past tense forms of these verbs are in the text. Find them.

regular: sail, ***sailed*** pull wait remain

irregular: be, ***was*** have build leave think become

Questions in the **past simple:**

Two nations were at war. ***Who were*** *they?*

What did *the Greeks* ***build****?*

Did *all the Greeks* ***sail*** *away from Troy?*

Negatives in the **past simple:**

The Trojans ***didn't know*** *that there were Greek soldiers inside the horse.*

The horse ***wasn't*** *a real horse and it* ***wasn't*** *a real gift.*

4 Work in small groups. Take each paragraph of the text in turn. Half of the group looks at the text and asks questions. The other half of the group answers without looking at the text.

Start like this: ***Two nations were at war. Who were they?***

5 Discuss these questions, giving reasons for your answers.

a Do you believe the story of the Trojan horse?

b Do you think the Statue of Liberty was a well-chosen gift?

c What is your opinion of the Fabergé egg as a gift?

1.3 What should I give?

In this lesson you will...

- listen to and understand information and opinions in a radio interview
- ask for and give ideas and opinions.

- **When do you give and receive gifts?**

Listening tip

Always read the questions before you listen.

Listening

05 **1** **Listen to two people talking on a radio programme. What are they talking about? Which country do they mention?**

2 **Listen again. Here are the interviewer's questions. How do Razia and Sandeep answer them?**

a What should you take when you visit friends and family?

b Should you be careful when giving flowers? Why?

c How should you wrap your gifts?

d When is money a suitable present?

e Is there anything you should remember when giving money?

f What do you give to close friends and family?

g When do you open your gifts?

h When do you exchange gifts?

Remember

You can use *should* and *shouldn't* to ask for and give advice.

*What **should** you take when you visit friends and family?*

***Should** you be careful when giving flowers?*

*You **should** wrap your gifts.*

*You **shouldn't** give white flowers.*

Speaking

3 **Work in groups. You're going to do a radio interview, like the one in Exercise 1.**

Step 1: Decide who is going to be the interviewer and who are going to be the guests.

Step 2: Ask and answer the questions in Exercise 2. Practise asking the questions with the correct pronunciation and intonation. Give your own answers to the questions.

Step 3: Do the interview. Use the words and phrases below.

Speaking tip

Make a note of the words and phrases below and use them whenever you can to keep a conversation going.

Useful phrases for expressing yourself

Give an opinion

I think it's always a good idea to (take / give) …

(Flowers / Sweets) … are good things to take for most occasions.

Make suggestions, ask about suggestions

You can also (take / give / send) …

You should never (give / take) …

You should wrap your presents in …

Why shouldn't you give …?

Give reasons

That's because …

Give examples

You may want to give special presents, like …

(At a wedding / When a baby is born), for example …

Add information

There's also a tradition of (giving / exchanging) …

Keeping the conversation going

Express agreement

Yes, I agree.

Ah, yes, good point.

Show you understand

Oh, I see.

Oh, right.

Comment on what someone has said

Ah, that's interesting.

1.4 You and your family

In this lesson you will...

- listen to a description of a family and write about your own family
- use apostrophes *'s* and *s'* (*my father's brother, my grandparents' early lives*).

- **In thirty seconds, how many words for family members can you remember?**

Vocabulary

1 **Work with a partner. Match the definitions to the words.**

ancestors	mother's mother	mother's father		
great-grandparents	nephew	niece	only child	relatives

a members of your family

b your brother's or your sister's daughter

c your brother's or your sister's son

d your grandmother on your mother's side

e your grandfather on your mother's side

f a child with no brothers or sisters

g your mother's / father's grandparents

h people in your family a long time ago

2 **Look at these informal words for members of the family. Who do they refer to?**

grandma	granny	grandpa	granddad	mum	dad

Speaking

3 **Work with a partner. Ask and answer these questions about your family.**

a What are your grandparents' first names? ***My mother's father is called …***

b Where were your grandparents born?

c Where were your parents born?

d What is your father's date of birth?

e How many cousins have you got? Can you name them all?

f Have you got any relatives you've never met?

g Have any members of your family emigrated to other countries? Who, and where?

h Do you know where your ancestors came from?

Use of English Apostrophes 's and s'

Notice the difference between apostrophe s ('s) and s apostrophe (s'):

- Apostrophe s ('s) shows that something belongs to one person or one thing
- s apostrophe (s') shows that something belongs to more than one person or thing.

What is your father's date of birth? = What is the date of birth of your father?

What are your grandparents' first names? = What are the first names of your grandparents?

Why is the apostrophe before the s in the first sentence and after the s in the second sentence?

4 Put the apostrophes in the right position in these sentences.

a My cousins name is Su-Wei.
My cousin's name is Su-Wei.

b My grandmothers name is Aisha.

c When I was young I lived very near my grandparents house.

d My sisters names are Grace and Alice.

e My fathers brothers live in Jakarta.

f I want to find out more about my ancestors lives.

Listening

5 Listen and answer the questions.

a Who has the same name as Alicia?

b Who was born first, Alicia or her brother Carlos?

c Where do Alicia's mother's parents live?

d Who are Rosa and Natalia?

e Where do Rosa and Natalia live?

f Are Rosa and Natalia on Alicia's mother's side or her father's side of the family? How do you know?

6 You've had an email from a distant relative who is researching your family history. Write your reply.

New message

Could you tell me anything you know about the family? What are your grandparents' names? Where were they born? Are you named after anyone in the family? I'd love to know about any relatives you have in other countries.

Looking forward to hearing from you.

Reply

Thank you for your email. Here is some information that might help you.

My (grandmother's/grandfather's) name is … . I'm named after my … . I've got an (older sister/younger brother). She's/He's called … . My mother/father is an only child. Some of my relatives live in …

1.5 Family history

In this lesson you will...

- read about people tracing their ancestors
- use *which/that, who* and *whose* in defining relative clauses.

Key words: Geography

Africa
Asia
China
Europe
Indonesia
south-east

- **Look at the words in the geography key words box. Which are continents? Which are countries? Which is a point of the compass?**

Reading

1 **Look at the map and read the article to find out about a scientific approach to family history. What does the map show?**

A remarkable journey

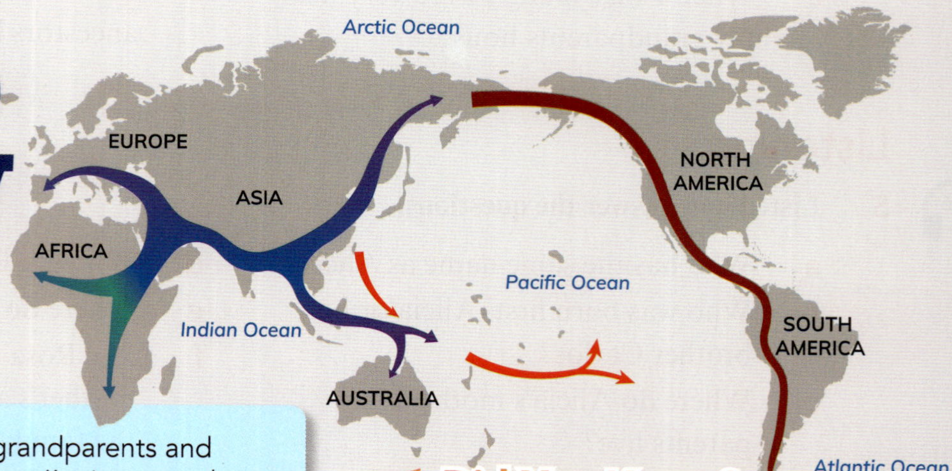

'I'm from Spain and my parents, grandparents and great-grandparents are Spanish too. I'm interested in family history, so I asked my parents to do a DNA test to find out about our ancestors. We discovered that our family history started in Africa. The DNA test showed that we're part of a family whose ancestors travelled from Africa through Europe to get here. It's a fascinating story. They were part of a group which also travelled as far east as China. I had no idea!' *Serena*

Did You Know?

DNA (deoxyribonucleic acid) is the hereditary material in humans and in almost all other living things. DNA is in the nucleus of the cells. It contains genetic information and instructions. What is 'DNA' in your language?

'I discovered that I'm descended from people who travelled across three continents. I wondered how they crossed from Asia into Alaska and then into Canada. I discovered there was once a land bridge that linked the two continents. That was more than 15,000 years ago. Amazing!' *Zak*

'I was surprised to find out that my ancestors travelled from Africa, through Asia and finally settled in South-East Asia, in Indonesia, where thousands of years later I was born. It's interesting to think that I share ancestry with people who live in countries far away. In a sense, they are my relatives, just like my cousins here in Jakarta. It made me think that we are all one big family!' *Vikal*

2 Answer the questions.

- a How did Serena find out about her ancestors? What did she find out?
- b How did Zak's ancestors reach Canada? Can people today make the same journey?
- c Where does Vikal live? Which route did his ancestors take to get there?
- d How do Serena, Zak and Vikal feel about their discoveries?

Use of English *which/that, who* and *whose* in defining relative clauses

Remember: *which / that* for things, *who* and *whose* for people.

There was once a land bridge. The land bridge linked the two continents.

There was once a land bridge ***which / that*** *linked the two continents.*

I share ancestry with people. Those people live in countries far away.

I share ancestry with people ***who*** *live in countries far away.*

I'm part of a family. Our ancestors travelled a long way to get here.

I'm part of a family ***whose*** *ancestors travelled a long way to get here.*

Why is it a good idea to join sentences together with *which / that, who* or *whose*?

3 Join these sentences together with *which / that, who* or *whose*.

- a You can do a DNA test. The test tells you where your ancestors came from.
  You can do a DNA test that (or ***which***) ***tells you where your ancestors came from.***
- b I've got some cousins and other relatives. They live in Italy.
- c Just over 8000 years ago there was a land bridge in Europe. The land bridge linked Britain to France.
- d I'm one of three Irish people in my class. Our ancestors all came from Limerick.
- e There are special websites and apps. These websites and apps help you find out about your family history.

Speaking

4 Work in pairs or groups. How would you explain to your parents or friends what you have learned from reading 'A remarkable journey'?

1.6 You and your school

In this lesson you will...

- listen to students talking about what they've done at school
- ask and answer questions about what you've done at school this term.

- **What are the main differences between your secondary school and your primary school?**

Reading

1 **A teacher has asked new students to describe their first few weeks at secondary school. Read what two of them said. Are they mostly positive or negative about their new school?**

2 **Answer the questions.**

a How long have Anisha and Felipe been at their new school?

b What has Anisha done outside lessons?

c What was difficult for Felipe at first?

d What went well for Felipe last week?

e What do you think Felipe means by 'so far, so good'?

My first few weeks at secondary school have gone well. I've enjoyed doing new subjects like chemistry. It's fun learning in a lab. I've also joined the school jazz band. I play the trumpet and we practise after school on Wednesdays. I've played volleyball, too. And I've made a lot of new friends.

Anisha

In the first week, I got into trouble when I was late for a lesson because I couldn't find the classroom. I've enjoyed English and I gave a presentation in history last week. It went well. I've played football but we haven't had any matches yet. I've got lots of new friends now. So far, so good!

Felipe

Use of English Present perfect simple

Present perfect simple	Past simple
We use the present perfect simple to talk about situations continuing up to the present. *Which subjects **have** you **enjoyed** this term?* *I**'ve enjoyed** science.* ***Has** the headteacher **spoken** to you?*	Remember, we use the past simple to talk about situations which have ended. *Which subjects **did** you **enjoy** last term?* *I **enjoyed** maths.*

We also use the present perfect when we don't specify a past time.
*What **have** you **done** in history? We**'ve done** the Ancient Greeks.*

3 **Complete the sentences using the present perfect of the verb in brackets.**

- a I've *made* *(make)* a lot of new friends this term.
- b I think we .... *(have)* too much science homework this term.
- c I .... *(enjoy)* new subjects like technology and design.
- d I'm in the football team, but we .... *(not play)* any matches yet.
- e My friend .... *(be)* in trouble with the headteacher.
- f .... you .... *(see)* the science labs? They're great!

Listening

4 **Before you listen, read the questions in the survey. Who do you think wrote the survey? Who is going to answer it?**

07 5 **Listen to Anisha and Felipe doing the survey. Have they done well at school this term?**

6 **How did Anisha and Felipe answer each question? Listen again.**

Class survey

This term ...

1 Which subjects have you enjoyed this term?

2 Which subjects have you enjoyed least?

3 What have you done in science?

4 What have you done in history?

5 Have you had good marks in all subjects?

6 Have you done any after-school activities?

7 Which sports have you played?

8 Have you been in trouble? And what for?

9 Has the headteacher spoken to you?

10 Have you enjoyed this term so far?

Speaking

7 **With a partner, ask and answer the questions in the class survey.**

Step 1: Partner A: Practise asking the questions in the survey with the correct pronunciation and intonation.

Partner B: Decide how you are going to answer the survey questions. Use the text in Exercise 1 and the answers to Exercise 3 to help you.

Step 2: Listen again to the conversation between Anisha and Felipe to help you.

Step 3: Ask and answer the questions in the survey.

1.7 Improve your writing

In this lesson you will…

- write an account of your first weeks at secondary school for the school website.

Follow these steps.

Step 1: **Work in groups. Discuss these questions.**

- Should the style be formal or informal?
- How long should your account be?
- Will it include photos or illustrations?

Step 2: **Write a plan for your account.**

On the opposite page there is a plan for you to follow.

Step 3: **Ask another student to check your plan.**

Step 4: **Write your account.**

Step 5: **Read through your account and check for mistakes.**

Pay attention to punctuation: are the apostrophes (') in the correct places?

Step 6: **Ask another student to read your account and comment on it.**

- Have you followed the plan on the opposite page?
- Is the information clear?
- Are the verb tenses correct (especially present perfect and past simple)?
- Have you used apostrophes correctly?
- Are there any spelling mistakes?
- Can you add anything to make it better?

Step 7: **Write a final version to be published on the school website.**

PARAGRAPH 1

General impressions

My first few weeks at secondary school have gone well.

The first few days

At first, ...

PARAGRAPH 2

School subjects and homework

My favourite subject is ...

It's fun (learning / doing) ...

In science / history we've ...

We've had quite a lot of homework in ..., but not much in ...

PARAGRAPH 3

Progress

I've had good marks in ...

I haven't done so well in ...

PARAGRAPH 4

After-school activities

I've joined ...

I've played ...

PARAGRAPH 5

Conclusion

I've enjoyed ...

I've learned ...

I've made some new friends.

All in all, I've ...

1.8 Project challenge

Project 1: Family history

You're going to write a profile of the oldest person in your family.

1 Read this account of an older family member. You're going to write something similar.

The oldest person in my family is my great-grandmother. She's my father's grandmother. Her name is Giulia. She's 96 and she was born in Naples, in Italy. She had seven brothers and sisters. When she was 18, she emigrated to Argentina with two of her brothers. She's lived here for 78 years and she's never been back to Italy, but she still speaks Spanish with an Italian accent! I've got some cousins and other relatives who live in Italy. I haven't met them, but I'd love to meet them one day.

Cecilia, Buenos Aires, Argentina

2 Think of an older member of your family.
Do some research to find out as much as you can about them.

- a What's his / her name?
- b How are you related to him / her?
- c How old is he / she?
- d Where was he / she born?
- e Does / Did this person have brothers and sisters?
- f Do you know anything interesting, amusing or surprising about him / her?

3 Write a profile of this person. Use Cecilia's profile of her great-grandmother to help you.

4 Work in groups. Other members of the group ask you the questions in Exercise 2. They can ask other questions if they want to.

- Was it useful to write an account of the family member before you answered the questions? Why?
- Did anybody ask you a question you couldn't answer? What did you say?

Project 2: A guide to social customs

You're going to design and write a guide to social customs for an exchange student visiting your school.

1 Work in groups. There are going to be two sections in the guide. Discuss the following questions and write down your ideas.

Section 1 Meeting and greeting

- What do you do when you meet someone for the first time? Are there different customs for greeting people of different ages?

  When you greet an older person, for example a grandparent, you ....

  When you meet an adult, you smile and shake hands. You shouldn't ....

- How should children address their teachers?

  They should call them ....

Section 2 Gifts

- What do visitors need to know about gifts?

  When you visit someone, you can take ....

2 Divide the work among the members of your group.

Who is going to write Section 1?

Shall we write Section 2?

Who wants to find the photos and illustrations?

3 Design and write your guide.

4 Exchange guides with another group. Make constructive comments and suggestions.

- How did working in groups help you?
- What did you learn from the comments of other students?
- Did you get ideas to improve your work from looking at other projects in the class? What were they?

1.9 Fiction

***To Give* by Vimal Shinagadia**

Vimal Shinagadia is 16 years old.

'My name is Vimal and I go to Whitefield School in London. This story is a traditional Hindi story and it was told to me by my friend's mother.'

08

1 **Read and listen to the first part of the story.**

Do you think the story is based on real events and real people? Or is it a fable – a traditional story that teaches a moral lesson? Give your reasons.

2 **Work in groups. Summarise this part of the story in no more than ten sentences.**

Step 1: Say what you remember of the key points of the story. Make sure every member of the group has a chance to say something.

Step 2: Choose one member of the group to write down the summary. Everyone in the group helps the person who is writing the summary.

Step 3: Each group takes it in turn to read their summary. The rest of the class listens to check that the details are correct.

3 **Answer these questions.**

a How would you describe the character of the king in this story?

b How would you describe the character of the peasant?

c Find four time expressions in the story. How do these time expressions help you when you're reading?

Once upon a time, …

4 **How many times does the writer use the word 'gold'? Why do you think he repeats the word?**

5 **Fables and traditional stories often feature an action that is repeated. What is the action in this part of the story that is repeated? Can you think of another traditional story where an action is repeated?**

6 **What do you think is going to happen next?**

- What is the king going to do?
- What is the peasant going to do?
- How is the story going to end?

[2] **generous:** wanting to help people by giving them money

[6] **gather:** to come together

[8] **peasant:** a poor farmer

[8] **crept:** (*past tense of creep*) moved quietly and carefully

[9] **huddle:** to move very close to

[18] **royal guard:** a person who protects a king or queen

[21] **thief:** a person who steals

[21] **steal:** to take what is not yours

[22] **capture:** to catch a person and keep them as a prisoner

[23] **prison:** a place where thieves and other criminals are kept

[29] **damp:** slightly wet

[30] **cell:** a small room in a prison where a prisoner is kept

[34] **gladly:** happily

[37] **fall on hard times:** to have little or no money and other difficulties in life

[40] **drought:** a long period of time when there is no rain

[41] **cattle:** cows

[58] **bestow:** (formal) to give someone an important present

To Give

Once upon a time, there was a very powerful and very generous king who gave much of his gold to the poor people of his lands. Each morning, the king would wake up early and share his gold with the poor people who had gathered at the gates of his palace so that they might buy food and clothing.

One night, a peasant crept up to the palace and huddled up against the wall where he would not be seen. The peasant decided that he would camp by the gates of the palace so that he would be the first in line to receive some gold pieces from the king the following morning. "If I am the first," reasoned the peasant, "then perhaps the king will give me more gold and I will no longer be poor or hungry."

But when one of the royal guards noticed the peasant creeping around at the gates of the palace, he thought that the man must be a thief come to steal the king's gold in the night. And so the guard captured the peasant and locked him away in the prison beneath the palace.

The next morning, after being told of the events of the previous night, the generous king decided to go and talk to the peasant who was locked in his prison.

The king approached the dark and damp cell and asked the peasant, "Why would you want to steal from me when all you had to do was ask for gold in order to feed and clothe yourself; do you not know that I would have given it to you gladly?"

The poor man explained that he was not a thief at all, but simply a peasant who had fallen on hard times and now needed help. "I was once a good farmer and a good businessman," said the man, "until the droughts came and thieves stole my cattle."

The peasant looked directly at the king. "I did not come to steal from you," he insisted. "I came in the night so that I might be the first to receive some gold in the morning. That is all, I promise."

Upon hearing the peasant's story, the generous king was much moved. He ordered the guards to release the man from his prison. Then he gave the peasant ten gold pieces with which to change his fortunes. The peasant thanked the generous king and left the palace with his gold.

But the next day, the peasant was not satisfied with his gift of ten gold pieces. Each night he returned to the palace and waited by the gates, and each morning the generous king bestowed upon the peasant ten more gold pieces.

This went on for many nights and many days, until the king asked the peasant, "Why do you continue to come to my palace when I have given you so much gold? Surely you are no longer poor or hungry?"

"But I wish to be like you," said the peasant to the king. "I want to be rich and powerful."

09

Turn the page to find out what happened.

"But will you also be generous to the poor of the land?" asked the king.

The peasant thought about this question for a few moments before he answered. "Yes, indeed I would, Your Majesty."

"Then I shall give you half of my kingdom and half of my riches," replied the king, "but you must promise me that you will always be generous to those who might need your help."

The peasant agreed, and so the king gave half of all his wealth and half of his entire kingdom.

The years passed quickly and the peasant proved to be a wise and generous man. He used much of his gold to plant food and raise cattle, and very soon he had doubled his riches and was able to share more and more wealth with the poor people of the land.

The king watched from his palace and was very pleased with what he saw. He knew then that to give was the greatest pleasure there ever was in the world. By sharing what he owned with others, the generous king was able to make many people happy. The peasant had learned this lesson well and he too shared his wealth and happiness with those around him. And very soon, because the king and the wise peasant both gave so generously, there was no more poverty or hunger in the whole of the land.

[76] **wealth:** money and possessions
[77] **entire:** whole, including everything
[78] **prove to be:** to show that you are (for example, wise and generous) after a period of time
[78] **wise:** intelligent because you have a lot of knowledge and experience
[83] **pleasure:** enjoyment
[84] **own:** to have (you own something that belongs to you)

7 Values Work in groups. Discuss these questions.

a Did you guess the end of the story correctly?

b How was your version of the end of the story different from the writer's version?

c What is the moral of the story? Do you agree with it? Give your reasons.

8 Choose one of the following scenes and imagine what the people in the story said to each other. Write a short dialogue.

Line 22	The royal guard captures the peasant.
Line 47–50	The king hears the peasant's story and releases him from prison.
	Imagine the peasant goes home and tells his family what has happened.

Check your progress

General knowledge quiz

How much can you remember about what you've learned?

1 What did the Greeks leave for the Trojans at the gates of their city, Troy? Why did they leave it there?

2 Look at the photo. What is it?

3 The Statue of Liberty was a gift from one country to another. Which were the countries?

4 What is at the feet of the Statue of Liberty?

5 What is a centenary?

6 In India, what colour flowers should you not give as a gift?

7 Put the letters in the correct order to make the names of three continents:

FARICA UPEORE IASA

8 It's in the nucleus of cells and it contains genetic information. What is it?

9 Alaska is part of the USA but it has a land border with which other English-speaking country?

10 How did people cross from Russia into Alaska more than 15,000 years ago?

Vocabulary

Meeting and greeting

1 **Make six phrases for meeting and greeting using the words in the circle.**
How are things?

are afternoon how
good morning later see you
nice to meet things

2 **Complete the phrases for meeting and greeting.**

a to n .... your head
b to b .... your head
c to sh .... hands
d to p .... your hands together

Family

3 **Complete the sentences.**

a I haven't got any brothers or sisters. I'm an .... child.
b My sister has got two children, a girl and a boy, so I've got a niece and a ....
c My mother's grandmother and grandfather are still alive, so I've got two ....
d My mum's from Colombia, so we've got cousins, aunts, uncles and other .... there.
e Thousands of years ago, some of our .... came from Scandinavia.

Use of English

1 Use the past simple of the verbs in the box to complete the text messages.

have	be	go	see	take

Last night, I ***went*** with my mum and dad to the cinema and we [1]________ a really good film. Afterwards we [2]________ ice creams. They [3]________ so colourful! I [4]________ this picture of them.

Great picture! Which cinema ***did you go*** to? What [5]________ the film about? How many ice creams [6]________ ? I went to the skating rink yesterday evening but I [7]________ you there. Now I know why!

2 Rewrite these sentences putting the apostrophe in the correct place.

- a My friends brother is a footballer. ***My friend's brother is a footballer.***
- b Our headteachers name is Mrs Smith.
- c Our science teachers names are Mr Hassan and Mrs Vidal.
- d My parents apartment is above their shop.

3 Use *which / that*, *who* or *whose* and the most suitable ending from the box.

- a The story is about a king
- b I've got a gold watch
- c In my class there's an Australian girl
- d This is a very interesting book

He gave a lot of money to the poor.
It tells you how to trace your family history.
It belonged to my great grandmother.
Her sister is a famous tennis player.

Summary checklist

I can

- ☐ talk about some customs of meeting and greeting.
- ☐ understand some descriptions of some famous gifts in history.
- ☐ talk about giving gifts.
- ☐ describe my family members and my family history.
- ☐ understand and talk about tracing ancestors.
- ☐ talk about my experiences at secondary school.
- ☐ have a conversation about giving gifts.

2 Time to celebrate

In this unit you will...

- **learn** about New Year celebrations
- **compare** three festivals
- **learn** about two spring festivals
- **describe** special occasions
- **learn** about early years traditions in Japan and parts of Africa
- **describe** April Fools' Day traditions
- **write** a description of an event for a partner school.

Getting started

"What are the important celebrations and family occasions in your country?"

Watch this!

2.1 Happy New Year!

In this lesson you will...

- learn about New Year celebrations
- use time phrases (*on New Year's Eve, at midnight, ...*).

- **Why do people celebrate New Year?**

Reading

1 **Work with a partner. Read the text and write a list of six words and short phrases that sum up Chinese New Year. Compare your lists.**

Chinese New Year is the most important celebration in the Chinese calendar. It is also known as the spring festival because it is the time when people welcome the arrival of spring. It celebrates the start of new life and the season for planting crops. It is the oldest Chinese festival.

New Year celebrations start when there is a new moon, on the first day of the lunar month in the Chinese calendar, in January or February (between 21 January and 20 February). Celebrations go on until the fifteenth day, when the moon is brightest.

Just before New Year, people clean their houses and throw away anything that is old or broken. They decorate their homes with pieces of paper with words such as 'happiness' and 'wealth' written on them. On New Year's Eve, families get together and have a special meal, which may include soup, fish, spring rolls, dumplings and rice cakes. People dress in red, which symbolises fire, and set off fireworks. Children receive gifts of money in red packets.

At the start of the first week of New Year, people visit friends and family. The second week ends with the Lantern Festival on the fifteenth day of the lunar month. People light lanterns to put in the windows of their houses. They walk in the streets carrying them under the light of the full moon.

One of the highlights of the Chinese New Year is the dragon dance. The dragons are made of paper, silk and bamboo. Chinese people think of dragons as helpful, friendly creatures which symbolise long life and wisdom.

Vocabulary

2 **Complete the table with words from the text.**

Nouns		welcome		decoration	symbol
Verbs	celebrate		arrive		

3 **Match the words from the text to the definitions.**

crops
lunar
fireworks
dragon
lantern
wisdom

a an imaginary creature that breathes fire
b a light that can be carried
c connected with the moon
d good sense and judgement based on experience
e plants like rice, corn or vegetables grown by farmers
f containers filled with powder that you light to produce a bang or bright colours

10 **4** **Listen to this description of New Year. Which country is it about? Which traditions are similar to Chinese New Year traditions?**

5 **Listen again. What can you remember about the New Year traditions in this country?**

Use of English Prepositions preceding nouns in time phrases

in January
on the first day of the lunar month
on New Year's Eve
at the start of the first week
at New Year
at midnight

Write the correct preposition to complete the rules.

Use .... with months, years and seasons.
Use .... with days and dates.
Use .... with clock times, festivals, *the weekend, the start / end of* ...

Language tip

Notice that we say '**on** Monday morning' but '**in** the morning'.

6 **Complete the sentences with the correct preposition.**

a Many festivals take place .... spring.
b We're going to decorate our house .... Saturday.
c Do they set off the fireworks in the afternoon or .... the evening?
d In Cuba, New Year's Eve is .... the end of December.

Speaking

7 **Work in groups. Talk about how you and your family celebrate New Year. Use these questions as a guide.**

a When do you celebrate New Year?
b What happens on New Year's Eve?
c What does your family do at New Year?

2.2 Three festivals

In this lesson you will...

- compare three festivals.

Key words: World religions

Buddhism
Catholicism
Christianity
Hinduism
Islam
Judaism
Sikhism

- **Name a festival. What does it celebrate?**

1 **Look at the words in the world religions key words box. Which five have the same suffix (a group of letters at the end of a word)?**

Reading

2 **The class is going to work in three groups. Each group reads about one of the festivals.**

Group A: Read about Diwali.

Group B: Read about Eid al-Fitr.

Group C: Read about Wesak.

3 **Look up in a dictionary any words you don't know.**

4 **Copy the chart into your notebook. Then complete your group's section of the chart.**

Group	Festival	Religion	When	How long	Key features
A	Diwali				
B	Eid al-Fitr				
C	Wesak				

Speaking

5 **In your group, take turns to ask other groups about their festivals. Ask these questions and complete the rest of your chart.**

a What's the name of your festival?

b Which religion celebrates it?

c When does it take place?

d How long does it last?

e What are the key features?

6 **Ask about any words you don't know.**

How do you spell 'rangoli'?

What are 'diyas'?

What is a 'courtyard'?

7 **Write captions for the photos of Eid al-Fitr and Wesak.**

Language tip

Remember to use the correct prepositions with time phrases:

***at** the end of October*

***in** April.*

Diwali

The word *Diwali* means 'rows of lighted lamps'. Diwali is the 'festival of lights' that celebrates the Hindu New Year. It is an important holiday in India and it is celebrated by communities around the world. The festival takes place at the end of October or the beginning of November. It lasts for five days. During the festival, people decorate their homes, courtyards, gardens and public places with small oil lamps called *diyas*. They draw brightly coloured *rangoli* patterns on the floor near the entrance to their houses. Fireworks are also an important part of the celebrations.

People light their homes with *diyas*

Rangoli is a traditional Indian decoration made from coloured rice, sand or flower petals

Eid al-Fitr

Eid al-Fitr celebrates the end of Ramadan in the Islamic world. Ramadan is the ninth month of the Islamic calendar. It's a time of fasting – going without food or drink during the day. The festival of Eid begins when the new moon is first seen in the sky.

Eid lasts for one, two or three days. The day starts with a small breakfast before people go to prayers at the mosque. After prayers, people visit their family and friends. Then there are special meals that may include meat, vegetable and rice dishes. There are usually a lot of sweet dishes, such as homemade halva and ice cream.

Wesak

The Buddhist festival of Wesak, or Vesak, is celebrated every year at the time of the full moon in April, May or early June. It lasts between a few days and a month. People wear white and visit their local temple. They take gifts of money, food, candles and flowers. They also take part in processions and they clean and decorate their homes. In Thailand and Indonesia, people carry lanterns made from paper and wood. Wesak is not only a time for celebration; it is also a time for reflection.

2.3 Welcoming the spring

In this lesson you will...

- learn about two spring festivals
- use compound adjectives in descriptions (*fur-lined, snow-covered, …*).

- **Write down three words or phrases that you think of when you picture a celebration. Compare your ideas.**

Reading

1 **Look at the picture on the right. What does it show? What's going to happen? Read the text to find out.**

Maslenitsa

The Russian festival of Maslenitsa takes place in February or March and lasts a week. It's a time to say goodbye to winter and to welcome the spring. At the beginning of the week, children make a large doll from straw and old clothes. This is Lady Maslenitsa, representing winter. The painting shows Maslenitsa a hundred years ago, with horse-drawn sleighs, snow-covered streets and people dressed in warm, fur-lined coats.

Today, Maslenitsa is still a time for having fun, and for eating *blinis*. These are small pancakes, made from eggs, butter and milk and served with butter, cream, jam, honey or caviar. Some people say they are a symbol of the sun, giving the earth warmth.

Maslenitsa also comes just before the period of Lent, when Christians traditionally give up rich foods. At the end of the week, the straw doll is burned on a bonfire. Winter is over and spring is on the way.

2 **Write five questions about Maslenitsa to ask your partner. Then ask and answer them.**

- a Where …?
  Where is Maslenitsa celebrated?
- b When …?
- c How long …?
- d What …?
- e Why …?

Use of English Compound adjectives

You can use two words together to make a compound adjective.

Sleighs that are drawn by horses are ***horse-drawn*** *sleighs.*

Streets that are covered in snow are ***snow-covered*** *streets.*

Coats that are lined with fur are ***fur-lined*** *coats.*

People who are dressed warmly are ***warmly dressed*** *people.*

Look back at the texts about Diwali in Lesson 2.2. Find a compound adjective. (Clue: it describes a pattern.)

3 **Complete the sentences using compound adjectives.**

- a Trees that are covered in frost are *frost-covered trees.*
- b Pancakes that are made at home are ………… .
- c A dome that is shaped like an onion is an ………… .
- d A blanket that is decorated beautifully is a ………… .
- e A day that is filled with fun is a ………… .

Speaking

4 **With a partner, talk about the Maslenitsa painting. Use the compound adjectives in Exercise 3 to describe what you can see.**

Listening

11 5 **Listen to this interview about a festival in South America, the carnival of Barranquilla. Which day of the festival is it?**

6 **Listen again and make notes about:**

- where and when the carnival takes place
- how long it goes on for
- the Battle of Flowers.

Writing

7 **Use your notes from Exercise 6 to write a description of the carnival of Barranquilla for a travel website. Try to include these compound adjectives:**

world-famous four-day second-largest brightly coloured

2.4 Special occasions

In this lesson you will...

- describe special occasions
- learn words and phrases to describe people's ages.

- **Which occasions do you celebrate in your family?**

Vocabulary and listening

Childhood	Teenage years	Adulthood
a child / children	a teenager / teenagers	an adult / adults
a baby (0–1)	in your early teens (12–14)	in your (early / mid- / late) twenties (20–29), thirties (30–39)
a toddler (1–2)	in your mid-teens (14–16)	middle-aged (40–60)
	in your late teens (16–19)	elderly (80+)

12

1 **Listen to Ella talking to her friend Lisa. What does Ella learn about Lisa? How much can you remember about what she says?**

2 **Listen again. Use the words and phrases in the vocabulary box to describe the ages of the family members.**

a Lisa's nephew *He's a baby.*
b Lisa's niece
c Lisa's brother
d Lisa's great-grandmother
e Lisa's parents

3 **Work in small groups. What's the age range of people in your family? Tell the group about them, starting from the youngest. Ask and answer questions to give more detail.**

My cousin's daughter is the youngest. She's a baby.

How old is she?

She's three months old.

13

4 **Listen to an interview with Lorena. Her sister is in the photo. What is she celebrating?**

5 **Listen again. Then answer the questions.**

a Where is Lorena from?

b At what age do people have a special birthday celebration in her country?

c Who is invited?

d What kind of occasion is it?

e Is it the same for girls and boys?

f How did Lorena's sister feel about her party and why?

Speaking

6 **Work in small groups. Look at the photo. What do you think it shows? Answer these questions.**

a What's the celebration?

b Who are the people? How are they related to each other?

c How old do you think they are? Use the expressions in the vocabulary box at the beginning of Lesson 2.4.

Compare your answers with the answers of other groups.

2.5 Starting out in life

In this lesson you will...

- learn about early years traditions in Japan and parts of Africa
- use *who*, *which* and *whose* in non-defining relative clauses.

Key words: Social studies

Swahili-speaking people

the Yoruba community

- **What were you like when you were baby?**

Reading

1 **Read about traditions associated with children around the world.**
How do you know that the traditions are important for members of the family?

A crying baby contest

In Japan, babies and toddlers between the ages of 6 months and 18 months take part in *nakizumo*. *Nakizumo*, which is a 400-year-old tradition, takes place once a year. The word *nakizumo* means 'crying baby sumo'. Two babies are placed on cushions on a stage with a referee. The referee, who sits between the babies, tries to make them cry. He tells them to '*nake, nake*' (cry, cry). The baby who cries the most is the winner.

The tradition is based on a Japanese proverb that says 'crying babies grow fast'. The event, which is held on Children's Day in Japan, is very popular with families. One of the organisers of the Tokyo event said: 'The father, the mother, the grandparents from both sides, they all seem to enjoy coming. It is truly a family event, sometimes even with all the other relatives. Everyone comes to the event and has a good time.'

Choosing a name

The birth name of a child among the Swahili-speaking people in Africa is used for the first 40 days of the baby's life. The name, which is chosen by an elderly relative, usually describes the baby's appearance or the circumstances at the time of their birth. Jamila, for example, means 'beautiful'. Chausiku means 'born at night'.

Babies who are born into the Yoruba community in Nigeria are also named according to the circumstances at the time of their birth. For example, Bejide means 'child born in the rainy time'. When they are a little older, the children are given a name to express hopes for the future. The success of the singer and songwriter, Ayodeji Ibrahim Balogun, whose name means 'twice the joy', is an example to show that these hopes can come true.

2 **Answer the questions.**

a What is happening in the picture?

b In the text, there are two examples of the way children's names are chosen in some African countries. What are they?

c Why do you think these traditions remain popular?

3 **Look at the words in the social studies key words box. Answer these questions.**

a What is Swahili and where is it spoken?

b Who are the Yoruba people and where do they live?

Use of English *which, who* and *whose* in non-defining relative clauses

Non-defining relative clauses give extra information in a sentence.

extra information
*Nakizumo, **which is a 400-year-old tradition**, takes place once a year.*

extra information
*The referee, **who sits between the babies**, tries to make them cry.*

extra information
*Ayodeji Ibrahim Balogun, **whose name means 'twice the joy'**, is an example to show that these hopes can come true.*

4 **Use a non-defining relative clause with *which, who* or *whose* to combine these sentences.**

a My friend Yannis has the same name as his cousin. Yannis lives in Athens.
My friend Yannis, who lives in Athens, has the same name as his cousin.

b Simba is a popular name in my country. It means 'lion'.

c My maternal grandfather was Spanish. He died before I was born.

d The name Kusuma means 'flower'. It comes from Sanskrit.

e My sister is always called 'Beth' at home. Her name is Elizabeth.

f The name Kadek is often given to the second child in Indonesia. It means 'younger brother or sister'.

Speaking

5 **Work in groups. Talk about the names in your family.**

a Do you have the same name as anyone in your family?

b Does your name have a special meaning? What about other members of your family?

c Which names are popular at the moment for boys and girls?

d Are there any names which sound old-fashioned now?

e Are there any traditions for celebrating a baby's birth or naming a baby in your country?

2.6 April Fools' Day

In this lesson you will...

- describe April Fools' Day traditions
- use participle adjectives (*amazed, amazing*) and idiomatic language (*by the way*).

- **The tradition of playing jokes on people and having fun at the beginning of spring comes from Persia and from Ancient Rome. Persia, which is now Iran, has the oldest known fun day, dating back to 536 BCE. Do you think a fun day is a good idea?**

Language tip

BCE is an abbreviation for 'Before the Common Era', so 536 BCE is over 2500 years ago.

Listening

14

1 **Listen to a conversation between Hasan and Zahra. What are they talking about? What day is it?**

2 **Work with a partner. What is the connection between each picture and April Fools' Day? Give as many details as you can.**

3 **Listen again. Then answer the questions.**

a What did Zahra think was **amazing**?

b Why was the newspaper story **interesting**?

c Why was Zahra **surprised** when she read about April Fools' Day in China?

d What wasn't very **exciting** for Zahra but was quite **amusing** for Hasan?

e At the end, Zahra said 'I'm **bored** with this now.' Was she really bored?

Use of English Participle adjectives ending in *-ed* and *-ing*

Look at the adjectives in **blue** in Exercise 3 and complete these rules.

Adjectives that end in .... describe how people feel. *(two examples)*

Adjectives that end in .... describe the thing that causes the feeling or a situation. *(four examples)*

4 **Choose the correct adjective in each sentence.**

a It was an *interested* / ***interesting*** story but I didn't believe it.
b We stayed up late last night, so we were really *tired* / *tiring* this morning.
c We got lost on our walk because the directions were *confused* / *confusing*.
d The film made me laugh. It was very *amused* / *amusing*.
e I was *amazed* / *amazing* to get such a good mark in my maths exam.

5 **Listen again. Put your hand up when you hear these idiomatic expressions.**

a **to fall for something** (*You fell for that one* / *people fell for it*) to think something is true when in fact it's not true
b **the wrong way round** something is the opposite of what it should be
c **Nice one!** an exclamation showing that something was well done
d **Guess what?** an exclamation to get the attention of someone when you want to tell them something interesting or exciting
e **to catch on** (*April Fools' Day is catching on*) to become popular
f **Hang on a minute** wait a moment
g **By the way** an expression you use to introduce a new subject or to give further information

Speaking

6 **Work in groups. Discuss these questions. Use the expressions in Exercise 5 if you can.**

a Is there a day in your country which is a 'fun day', like April Fools' Day? When is it? What do people do? If there isn't a fun day in your country, do you think there should be? Why?
b Have you ever played an April Fools' Day type of trick on someone? What was it? Did the person fall for it? What was the person's reaction? What do other people in the group think about it?

2.7 Improve your writing

In this lesson you will...

- write a description of an event for a partner school.

1 **Read the description of an event on the opposite page. What is the writer's intention? Has she succeeded?**

2 **Remember that you can use participle adjectives ending in *-ing* to express your feelings about what you're describing.**

Find three *-ing* adjectives in the text.

Here are some more adjectives you can use when you do Exercise 4: *amazing, astonishing, interesting, surprising*.

3 **You can also use compound adjectives, to add colour and detail.**

How are the dresses described in the text?

Here are some more compound adjectives you can use when you do Exercise 4: *home-baked (bread), hand-made (costumes), pale-blue (shirts)*

4 **Write a description of a celebration, festival or traditional event in your country for a partner school in another country. Use the description on the opposite page as a model.**

- In paragraph 1, have you answered the questions *When? Where? Why?*
- In paragraph 2, have you used time expressions?
- Have you used a relative clause with *which* to give extra information?
- Have you included one or more adjectives ending in *-ing*?
- Have you included one or more compound adjectives?

Writing tip

Non-defining relative clauses are more often used in written English than in spoken English.

Afterwards, we have a special cake called a coca, ***which has fruit and sugar on top***.

Using them to combine sentences shows that you have a good command of written English.

Choose a title.

Paragraph 1
When? Where? Why?

Paragraph 2
What happens?
You can use time expressions such as *first*, *next*, *later*, *afterwards* to show the sequence of events.

Paragraph 3
Add more detail. You can use relative clauses with *which* to give extra information.

Paragraph 4
Give a personal point of view.

Paragraph 5
Conclusion

A village festival

Every year in June there are celebrations throughout the country to mark the middle of summer. This is the festival of San Juan and it takes place on the Saturday nearest to midsummer.

In our village, everyone gets together to join in the fun. First, some of the children take turns to read out a traditional poem. The most exciting moment is when the big bonfire is lit. Next, we let off fireworks. This can be a bit frightening because some of the fireworks make a lot of noise.

Later, we all sit down around big tables in the village hall for a special meal. The barbecue, which is served by the mayor of the village and his helpers, includes chicken, sausages and other meat. Afterwards, we have a special cake called a *coca*, which has fruit and sugar on top. After the meal, we go outside again for singing and dancing. The older children keep an eye on the younger ones to make sure they don't get near the fire.

My sister and I are in the village choir, so when it's time for us to sing, we get dressed up in our traditional costumes. The girls and the women wear brightly coloured dresses and the boys and men wear red scarfs and white shirts. The songs aren't all serious; in fact, some of them are quite amusing.

San Juan gives all the families and neighbours a chance to chat and catch up. Everyone has a good time.

2.8 Project challenge

Project 1: Celebrations and traditions

You're going to give a short presentation about traditional ways of celebrating the birth of a baby and welcoming him or her to the family and community.

1 What are the traditions in your country?

2 Find out about these traditions in other countries:

France – toy giraffe called 'Sophie'

Germany – planting a tree

Netherlands – stork announces birth

Nigeria – grandmother gives baby his or her first bath

Sweden – silver spoon for the baby

3 Prepare your presentation. Here is an example to help you.

The Hundred Days Party is a tradition in China. Family and friends get together to celebrate the baby's first hundred days and to wish that he or she will live for a hundred years. Then, when the baby is a year old, there is another tradition. The baby is offered a tray of objects, such as a paintbrush, a book, money or medicine, which represent a variety of professions. It's an exciting moment. Everybody is intrigued to know what the baby will be most interested in. If the baby picks up the paintbrush, for example, he or she might become an artist.

4 Give your presentation.

- What did you learn from looking up information for this project?
- How did you use the model text?

Project 2: A festival poster

You're going to produce an information poster about a festival.

1 Work in small groups. The picture shows the Songkran festival in Thailand. What's happening? Describe the picture.

2 In your groups, look up these festivals on the internet. Which do you find the most interesting?

Songkran (Thailand)

Carnival (Brazil, Italy, etc.)

St John's Eve (Scandinavia)

The Moon Festival (China)

Setsubun (Japan)

The Lemon Festival (Menton, France)

3 Discuss which festival you're going to choose for your poster.

> I like the sound of ..., because ...

> What about ...? We could get some good pictures to illustrate it.

4 Find the answers to these questions.

a When and where is the festival celebrated?
b What does it celebrate?
c How long does it last?
d What happens during the festival?
e What special events are there?
f What do people eat during the festival?

5 Decide how to plan, organise and produce the work.

a Who is going to design the poster?
b Who is going to find the pictures?
c Who is going to do the illustrations?
d Who is going to write the text?

6 Make the poster. Then use it to give a presentation to the rest of the class.

- What did you learn from looking up information for this project?
- How did you decide which festival to present?

2.9 Poetry

1 Read and listen to the poem. If this was a video clip, what would you see?

Tuen Ng (The Dragon Boat Races)

The air is hushed
round waiting boats;
water still before the race.
Slowly paddles lift
above the dragon-prows
like giant wing-bones
from a waking beast,
stretching into space …

And then …
they're off!
Away!

Fish scatter in dismay
as dragon-racers slice the surface.
Wings dip, whip water into waves;
waves rise like flames,
set light by sun.

Above, flags tug at their fetters,
desperate to join the fun.
And all around,
like pumping, thumping dragon-hearts,
the pounding gongs,
the beating drum.

Judith Nicholls

[1] hushed: very quiet
[4] paddle: a short pole with a flat end that you use to make a small boat move through the water
[5] prow: the front of a boat
[7] beast: an animal, especially a dangerous or strange one
[8] stretch: to reach as far as possible
[12] scatter: to move away in different directions
[12] dismay: a feeling of unhappiness and disappointment
[13] slice: to cut as if with a knife
[14] dip: to lower something into a liquid and then take it out again
[14] whip: (here) to hit the water quickly to cause waves
[15] flame: the brightly burning gas that you see coming from a fire
[17] tug: to pull something quickly and with a lot of force
[17] fetters: chains for a prisoner's feet
[20] pumping: forcing liquid to move
[20] thumping: beating fast (so that you can feel it)
[21] pounding: being hit repeatedly
[21] gong: a round piece of metal which is hit with a stick to make a sound

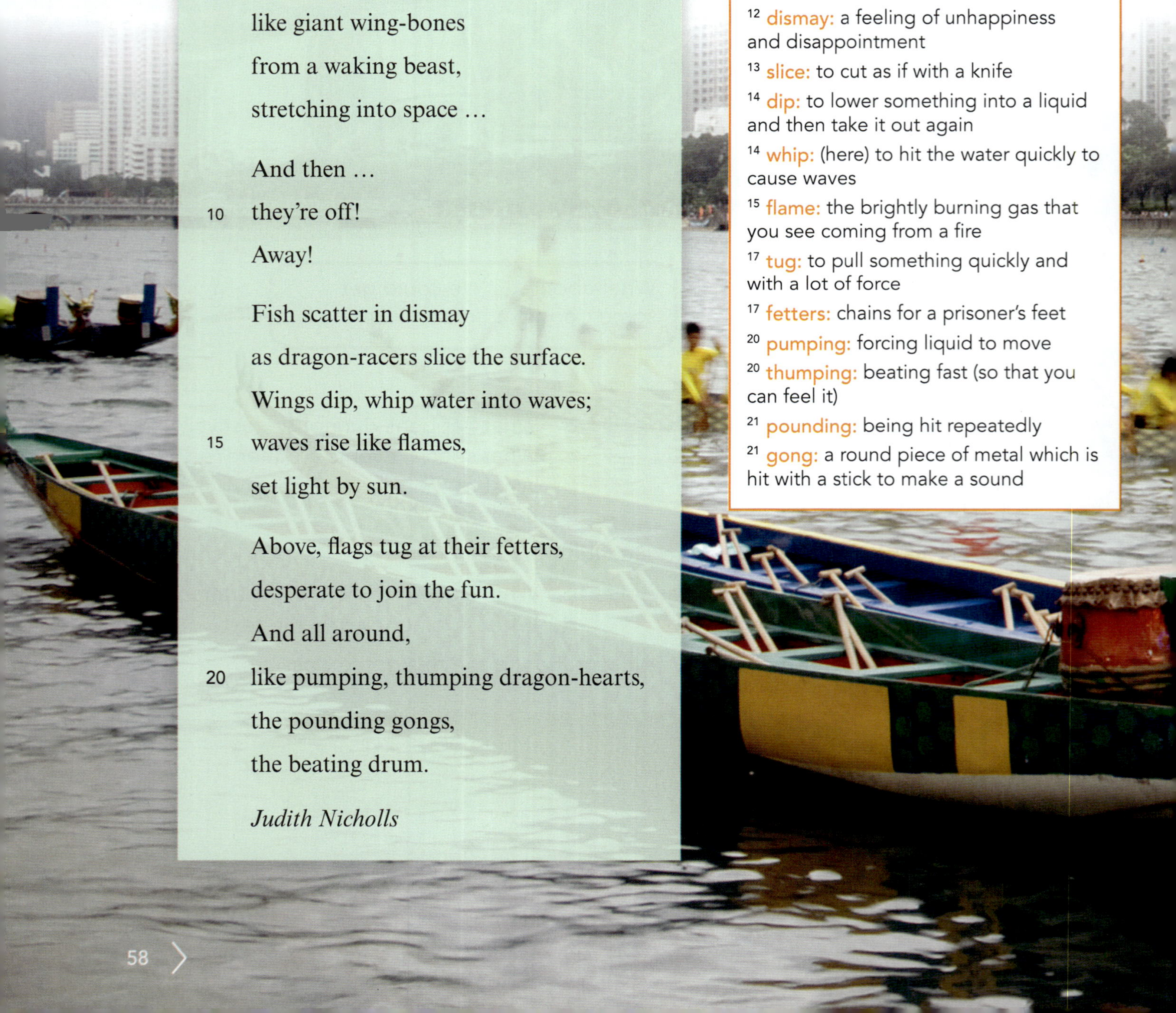

2 **Read and listen to the poem again. Then answer the questions.**

- **a** What is the difference between the first verse and the rest of the poem?
- **b** Why is the second verse so short?
- **c** What do you **see** in the third verse?
- **d** What do you **hear** in the fourth verse?

3 **Read the description of four poetry techniques in the Language tip. Find one example of each in verses 3 and 4.**

Onomatopoeia: the word 'thump' sounds like the action of thumping something.

Language tip

Onomatopoeia is when a word sounds like the sound it describes, like the ***buzz*** of a bee.

Alliteration is when you use the same sound at the beginning of several words in a line: a ***f***antastic ***f***un-***f***illed ***f***estival.

A **simile** shows the similarity of one thing to another, using the words *like* or *as*: she ran ***like*** the wind.

Personification means talking about a thing as if it were a person: the wind ***whistled*** through the trees.

16

4 Read and listen to the second poem. If this was a video clip, what would you see?

Chinese New Year Dragon

There's a brightly coloured dragon swaying down the street,
Stomping and stamping and kicking up its feet.

There's a multicoloured dragon – green, gold and red –
Twisting and twirling and shaking its head.

There's a silky-scaled dragon parading through the town,
Swishing and swooshing and rippling up and down.

There's a swirling, whirling dragon, weaving to and fro,
Prancing and dancing and putting on a show.

There's cheering and clapping as the dragon draws near –
A sign of good luck and a happy new year!

John Foster

[1] sway: to move slowly from side to side
[2] stomp, stamp: to put your foot down on the ground hard and quickly
[4] twist: to turn part of your body to face a different direction
[4] twirl: to turn around and around quickly
[6] swish: to move quickly through the air making a soft sound
[6] swoosh: to make the sound of fast-moving air
[6] ripple: to move in small waves
[7] swirl, whirl: to move quickly in circles
[7] weave: to make a path by moving quickly and changing direction often
[8] prance: to walk or dance in a proud way, often because you want people to look at you

5 Look at the words in the glossary. What do they all describe?

6 Answer these questions.

What do you notice about …

- a the last words in each line?
- b the rhythm? (Does it have a strong regular beat?)
- c the use of adjectives? Are there any compound adjectives?

7 Values Work with a partner. Practise reading the poem aloud. Take turns to read a line each.

8 Give a class performance of the poem.

Check your progress

General knowledge quiz

How much can you remember about what you have learned?

1. At Chinese New Year, what colour do people wear? What does it symbolise?
2. In Cuba at New Year, what do people eat at midnight?
3. Which religions are associated with the following festivals: Diwali, Eid al-Fitr, Wesak?
4. In which country and at what time of year does Maslenitsa take place?

5. In which country is there a 400-year-old tradition called *nakizumo* and what is it?
6. Name a country where a girl has a special party to celebrate her 15th birthday.
7. On which continent is Nigeria?
8. What was Iran called in the past?
9. What date is April Fools' Day?
10. In which country do people put a paper fish on someone's back on April Fools' Day?

Vocabulary

Festivals

1 Fill in the missing words. Then choose either the verb or the noun to complete the sentences.

verbs	nouns
to *welcome*	a welcome
to celebrate	a ....
to	a dance
to decorate	a ....
to	a light
to symbolise	a ....

a Some people say Russian blinis are *a symbol* of the sun.

b People .... Chinese New Year in January or February.

c The dragon .... is one of the highlights of Chinese New Year celebrations.

d During the festival of Diwali, people .... their homes and .... small oil lamps called *diyas*.

Ages and stages

2 Match the ages to the stages.

1	0–1	a	elderly
2	1–2	b	in your early teens
3	13–14	c	a toddler
4	14–16	d	in your late teens
5	16–19	e	in your twenties
6	20–29	f	in your mid-teens
7	40–60	g	a baby
8	Over 80	h	middle-aged

Use of English

1 Use *in*, *on* or *at* to complete the time phrases in these sentences.

The Moon Festival

In China, the Moon Festival takes place ***in*** autumn, __________ [a] the end of September or the beginning of October.

It is celebrated __________ [b] the 15th day of the 8th month in the Chinese calendar, on the night of a full moon. The Moon Festival was made a Chinese public holiday __________ [c] 2008.

2 Make compound adjectives from these words to use in the sentences below.

horse	covered	home
drawn	brightly	coloured
snow	made	

a We rode in a ***horse-drawn*** sleigh.

b There were lots of delicious .... dishes.

c The decorations were made of .... paper.

d We saw .... mountains from the plane.

3 Add the appropriate extra information from the box to the middle of each sentence, using *which*, *who* or *whose*.

It's a city in Colombia.
It's held in February or March.
She lives in Germany.
It's on the top floor.
Her parents are from Kenya.

a Our room has a view of the city.
Our room, which is on the top floor, has a view of the city.

b My sister is a civil engineer.

c The carnival attracts visitors from all over the country.

d Cartagena has an international film festival.

e Rosa speaks both English and Swahili fluently.

Summary checklist

I can

- ☐ give and understand descriptions of New Year celebrations, and describe a New Year celebration.
- ☐ talk about festivals celebrated around the world.
- ☐ describe a painting in detail.
- ☐ describe people in terms of their age group.
- ☐ discuss early years traditions in Japan and parts of Africa.
- ☐ describe April Fools' Day traditions.

3 What we wear, what we waste

In this unit you will...

- **use** vocabulary for clothes and parts of clothes, and use verbs to do with clothes
- **learn** about clothes, accessories and materials from the past
- **talk** about clothes and their significance
- **discuss** ways of protecting the environment using modal verbs and *have (got) to, ought to, need to*
- **find out** how waste materials can be reused
- **give** a short speech about an environmental problem
- **write** a letter about an important local issue.

Getting started

"We shouldn't buy so many clothes. Do you agree?"

Watch this!

3.1 My style

In this lesson you will…

- use vocabulary for clothes and parts of clothes, and use verbs to do with clothes
- use multi-word verbs (*put on*, *do up*, *try on*) to talk about what you wear.

- **What sort of clothes and shoes are in fashion at the moment?**

Clothes

hooded sweatshirt / a hooded jacket (often called a 'hoodie')
polo shirt
tracksuit bottoms
designer jeans
short-sleeved shirt
knee-length shorts

Parts of clothes

button collar
hood lace(s)
(long / short) sleeve(s)

Vocabulary

1 **Read what Joshua says about clothes.**

What is Joshua wearing in the photo? Use the words from the box to help you.

When I get home after school, I just put on something comfortable like tracksuit bottoms and an old T-shirt. I don't like clothes with lots of buttons to do up. I don't like shoes with laces either. I don't mind trainers but I leave the laces done up so I can just slip them on.

I don't enjoy shopping for clothes because I don't like trying things on in a shop. I don't really need a lot of clothes. Who does? I just like wearing things that look good on me. I'm quite careful with my clothes. When I go to bed, for example, I don't just take them off and throw them on the floor. I fold them and put them away or hang them up in the wardrobe.

When I go out with my friends, I usually wear jeans with a T-shirt and sometimes a polo shirt. I don't mind dressing up for family weddings and things like that, but I don't really follow fashion.

Joshua

Use of English Multi-word verbs (phrasal and prepositional verbs)

Multi-word verbs are verbs made up of two or more words – a verb like *get* or *take* with a word like *up* or *off*.

How many multi-word verbs can you find in the text in Exercise 1?

put on, do up, slip on, …

When the object of a multi-word verb is a noun, you can put the two words of the verb together or you can separate them.

But if the object is a pronoun, you must separate the two words.

*I **put away** my clothes.*	*I **put** them **away**.*
OR	NOT
*I **put** my clothes **away**.*	~~*I put away them.*~~

2 **Use the words in the box to complete the multi-word verbs in the following questions. Then ask and answer them with a partner.**

on (x2)	off	for	up	away

a Do you ever pay …*for*….. your own clothes?

b Do you always try clothes ……….. before you buy them?

c Do you like dressing ……….. for special occasions?

d Do you always put your clothes ……….. in the same order?

e When you take your clothes ……….. at the end of the day, do you put them ……….. carefully?

Writing

3 **Rewrite what Joshua says in Exercise 1 to make it true for you.**

Listening

7 4 **Listen to this interview with Amani and Milan. What are they talking about? Do they have similar opinions?**

5 **Listen again. Put your hand up when you hear these sentences. Can you say each of the underlined phrases in a different way?**

a I often <u>go window-shopping</u>.

b I try on different pairs of shoes to see which ones <u>go well with</u> it.

c Are you <u>fashion-conscious</u>?

d Do you dress up for special occasions? <u>Not if I can help it</u>!

6 **Answer the questions. Who …**

a enjoys shopping and trying on clothes?

b isn't interested in fashion?

c buys a lot of clothes?

d has an untidy bedroom?

e shops online?

f are you most likely to see in family photos?

Speaking

7 **Work in groups. Discuss your attitude to clothes. In what ways are you similar to or different from Joshua, Amani and Milan?**

3.2 How stylish were the Ancient Egyptians?

In this lesson you will…

- learn about clothes, accessories and materials from the past.

- **What do you know about the Ancient Egyptians?**

Key words: History

emperor
hieroglyph
pharaoh
status

Reading

1 **Look at the words in the history key words box. Use them to complete these sentences.**

a An ……….. was a ruler in China.

b A ……….. was a ruler in Ancient Egypt.

c A ……….. is a picture or symbol which is used to represent a word or part of a word in the Ancient Egyptian writing system.

d Your ……….. is your social position in relation to other people.

2 **What clothes did the Ancient Egyptians wear? What else did they wear? Read the text to find out.**

Clothing and footwear

In Ancient Egypt, the most popular material for clothes was linen. The women wore long, straight dresses. The men wore skirts with a belt. Both men and women wore make-up and jewellery. Only the pharaoh and people of high status had footwear. They wore sandals with leather straps. Colours were symbolic for the Egyptians. Yellow symbolised gold, green was the symbol of youth and life, black was only for wigs and white was the symbol of happiness.

Jewellery

People have always worn jewellery to show off their status, for decoration, for practical purposes, or just for fun. In Ancient Egypt, everyone wore jewellery, not just the rich and powerful. They liked to use gold for their bracelets, rings, earrings, decorated buttons and necklaces. In the picture, the Egyptian woman is holding an object in the shape of an Egyptian hieroglyph, the 'ankh', which is a symbol of life.

3 **Find the following in the text.**

a one type of footwear ***sandals***

b two items of clothing

c four items of jewellery

4 **Are these sentences true or false?**

a Ancient Egyptians wore a lot of linen.

b Only women wore skirts.

c Men wore make-up.

d Everyone wore sandals.

e Yellow and green were important colours for the Ancient Egyptians.

f The Egyptians liked wearing black clothes.

g All Egyptians had some items of jewellery.

h The *ankh* had a negative meaning for the Egyptians.

Speaking

5 **Discuss these questions.**

a What similarities are there between the Ancient Egyptians and people today?

b Can you tell what the attitude of the writer is in this text? (In other words, can we say what the writer's opinion is, or does the text simply give the facts?)

Listening

18

6 **Listen to part of a talk given by a museum guide. What is the talk about? How does it link to the text about Ancient Egypt?**

Writing

7 **Listen again. Answer these questions. Then use the words in the history key words box to summarise what the museum guide says.**

a What was a status symbol in Ancient China?

b What material did poor people make their clothes from?

c Who wore silk?

d What colour did the emperor wear?

e What was the important item of jewellery for men?

Listening tip

When you summarise what you read or what you hear, you need to focus on the main points. The questions in Exercise 7 will help you do this. Read them before you listen again.

Key words: History

buckle
emperor
hemp
silk
status symbol

3.3 Clothes and you

In this lesson you will…

- talk about clothes and their significance
- use idiomatic expressions to talk about clothes.

- **'You are what you wear.' Is this true?**

Reading, listening and speaking

1 **Read the questions in the quiz on the next page, but don't answer them yet.**

The quiz has three parts. Which is the easiest part to answer? Which is the most challenging? Give reasons for your answers.

19

2 **Listen to Lian and her brother answering the questions in Part 1 of the quiz. Which of the following multi-word verbs do they use?**

put on	put away	try on	pay for	take off

3 **With a partner, ask and answer the questions in Part 1 of the quiz. Try to use some of the expressions Lian and her brother use.**

… a waste of time

I quite enjoy it.

It's nice to …

You need to know whether you look good in [them].

I don't mind [dressing up].

Natural materials
linen
wool
cotton
silk…

Synthetic materials
plastic
polyester
rayon
acrylic…

20

4 **Listen to Lian and her brother answering the questions in the Part 2 of the quiz. What are these, and who wears them?**

1

2

5 **Now ask and answer the questions in Part 2 of the quiz. Use the present passive (*It's made of …*) in your answers.**

6 **With a partner, ask and answer the questions in Part 3 of the quiz.**

Remember

Present passive

*What **is** it **made** of?*

*It**'s made** of metal.*

Clothes and you

PART 1 Are you fashion conscious?

1 Do you enjoy shopping for clothes?

2 Do you always try clothes on before you buy them?

3 Do you like dressing up for special occasions?

PART 2 How much do you know about the clothes you wear?

4 Describe what you're wearing.
Do you know what each item is made of?

5 Do you wear jewellery? What is it made of?

6 Do you wear other accessories (a belt, for example)?
What are they made of?

PART 3 Think about it.

7 Why are clothes important to people?

8 What are the advantages and disadvantages of natural materials for clothes?

9 What are the advantages and disadvantages of synthetic materials?

3.4 Think globally, act locally

In this lesson you will...

- learn vocabulary for environmental issues
- discuss ways of protecting the environment using modal verbs and *have (got) to, ought to, need to.*

- **What does 'think globally, act locally' mean to you?**

1 **Look at the words in the box. Can you complete what each person says about thinking globally and acting locally?**

Environment
carbon
climate
emissions
environmental
fashion
pollution
recycle
waste

I think it means you should think about things like air and water ...., things that affect everyone.

I watched a programme about how much we throw away.

We all need to reuse and .... more.

Claudia

You've got to think about the problems in the world: .... problems, like .... change.

Eliud

Take the .... industry. I read that it produces 1.7 billion tonnes of .... dioxide every year and it is responsible for about 10 per cent of global carbon ....

So many clothes are worn only a few times and then thrown away. It's a terrible ....!

Raina

Listening

21 2 **Listen to these extracts from an interview with the people in the photos. Check your answers to Exercise 1.**

22 **3 Listen to the complete interviews. Which sentence summarises what all the people in the photos say?**

- **a** It's not for us to decide how to solve the problems. Governments and politicians should do that.
- **b** It's too late to stop climate change.
- **c** There are things we can all do to make a difference.

Language tip

Useful multi-word verbs for this topic

cut down on: reduce

throw away: get rid of (*the opposite of keep*)

find out: discover, get information

4 Listen again. Claudia, Eliud and Raina give examples of ordinary things we can all do to be environmentally friendly. What are they?

a Claudia ***Always use …*** **b** Eliud **c** Raina

Use of English Modal verbs and *have (got) to, ought to, need to*

strong obligation: must will have (got) to

*You've **got to** think about the problems in the world.*

weak obligation should ought to might

*You **should** think about things like pollution.*

necessity don't have to needn't need to

*We all **need to** recycle more.*

possibility: can could may might

*We **might** be able to slow down climate change*

prohibition must not can't

*You **must not** buy so many clothes.*

suggestion should shall

*What **should** we do about this?*

23 **5 Work in pairs. Use statements 1–4 as the basis for four conversations. (You can listen to two model conversations to help you.)**

Statements	Useful phrases for conversational exchanges		
1 We must cut down on the things we use every day. 2 We have to change the way we think about clothes and fashion. 3 We could cycle more instead of going everywhere by car. 4 We all need to recycle more.	Why? Yes, but what can we do / how do we do that? What do you mean? Give me an example. That's a good idea but …	Because … For example, … I mean … Yes, but … Well, I think we have to …	I see what you mean. Yes, I agree. No, I don't agree.

3.5 Don't waste it!

In this lesson you will...

- find out how waste materials can be reused
- use the present passive with modals (*shoes can be made from plastic bottles*).

- **Think of your everyday clothes. What are they made of?**

Key words: Science

- algae
- foam
- habitat
- raw materials

Reading

1 **Read the article and answer the questions.**

a What is the writer's intention in this article?

b Can we say what the writer's opinion is, or does the text simply give the facts?

Plastic Plus

Eight million tonnes of plastic are thrown into the oceans each year. This means that by 2050, there will be more bits of plastic than fish in seawater. What can be done?

Did you know that sportswear, such as jackets, swimwear, leggings, trainers, T-shirts and bags can be made from recycled plastic found in oceans and rivers? The plastic is broken down into pellets and then the pellets are made into thread. The thread is used to make material for clothes. This process is called 'upcycling' because you're recycling waste material to make something new, which is good news for the environment. Some people define upcycling as 'creative reuse'.

There's a Spanish fashion company that makes shoes from waste plastic and algae. Each pair of shoes is made from five plastic bottles. The plastic is processed into thread for making cloth. The thread is used to make the upper part of the shoe. Algae are processed into a flexible foam material to make the base of the shoe. The shoes are simple and comfortable, they can be produced easily and they look very stylish.

It's a win-win situation because removing the algae also allows clean water in rivers and lakes to circulate more freely, which helps to improve plant and animal habitats.

A Plastic water bottles are collected.

B The bottles are broken down into pellets, which are made into thread.

C The thread is used to make fabric for clothes.

2 Look at the words in the science key words box. Match them to their definitions.

- a a lot of bubbles that stick together on the surface of a liquid
- b materials in their natural state, like wood, coal and oil
- c natural home of a plant or animal
- d small plants with no stems or leaves that grow in or near water

3 Work in groups. Discuss the questions.

- a What can recycled plastic be used for?
- b Why is upcycling sometimes called 'creative reuse'?
- c Can natural and synthetic materials be combined to make shoes? Give an example from the text.
- d Why does the article say this is a 'win-win situation'?

Language tip

made from* and *made of

Use *made from* if the original material has been completely changed.

These shoes are ***made from*** *recycled plastic.*

Use *made of* if you can still recognise the original material.

These shoes are ***made of*** *leather.*

Use of English Present passive with modal verbs

You can use modal verbs like *can, could, should* and *must* with the present passive.

The shoes ***can be produced*** *easily.*

Plastic ***shouldn't be thrown*** *into the sea.*

Can *these shoes* ***be recycled****?*

4 Complete these sentences using the present passive.

- a Oil .... under the earth and under the sea. (*find*)
- b Too many empty plastic bottles .... into the ocean. (*throw*)
- c Diamonds .... at high temperatures deep underground. (*form*)
- d Belts .... of materials such as leather, plastic or cotton. (*can / make*)
- e Baseball caps and sunglasses .... in the classroom. (*must / not / wear*)
- f .... all plastic waste .... in the recycling bin? (*should / put*)

Speaking

5 Work in groups. Answer these questions.

- a What sort of things are recycled in your country?
- b Are there other things that should be recycled?
- c Can you think of something you've got at home that could be upcycled?

3.6 Reduce, reuse, recycle

In this lesson you will...

- give a short speech about an environmental problem.

- **Reduce, reuse, recycle: what do these words mean in the context of the environment?**

Reading

1 **Read the article on the opposite page. Who are the young people in the pictures? Where are they? Why are they there?**

Listening and speaking

24

2 **Listen to the data about waste. Complete the sentences with the correct numbers from the box.**

half	95	2050	billion
5	500	100,000	

a Around a trillion bags are used every year worldwide. A single plastic bag can take *500* years or more to degrade.

b By........... the oceans will contain more plastic by weight than fish.

c Over .... marine animals die every year from getting caught in plastic or from eating it.

d Over one third of all food produced globally goes to waste. One .... hungry people could be fed on a quarter of the food that is thrown away every year.

e More than .... of all food that is wasted is thrown away at home.

f Up to .... % of the textiles that are thrown away could be recycled.

g It only takes .... recycled plastic bottles to make enough fibre filling for one ski jacket.

Listening tip

Before you listen, look at the gaps in the sentences. What kind of numbers do you expect to hear?

Language tip

A ***single*** plastic bag means ***just one*** plastic bag.

3 **Work in pairs. Ask each other three questions about the information in Exercise 2.**

- How many ...?
- How much ...?
- How long ...?
- What will happen ...?
- Why ...?
- What percentage ...?

4 Imagine you're going to attend the next Youth and Future Generations Day. You have to give a short speech about an environmental problem that concerns you.

a You've only got 20 seconds to get your message across. What are you going to say?

b Think about the following:

- Can you use any of the information in Exercise 2 to support your message?
- Do you need to do some research to find other information?
- Can you use any of the stylistic devices Timoci and Shalvi used?

c Write down what you're going to say.

d Practise what you're going to say.

e Give your speech.

Every year, young people from around the world are invited to take part in the Youth and Future Generations Day, organised by the United Nations Climate Change Conference. Timoci and Shalvi spoke at the recent conference in Bonn, Germany.

“We need to act now. Therefore, let's start with putting rubbish in the bin. Reduce, reuse and recycle. Let's replant. Let's be more environmentally oriented ... It's time to unite, to move forward ... Climate change is here to stay unless we do something about it.”

Timoci Naulusala

“A famous activist, Emma Thompson, said, 'Every single person on this earth has the power to change the world.'

Plant a tree. Walk instead of taking a car for a short distance. Our school has opted for an action plan, which is to plant trees and have three Rs: Reduce, Reuse, Recycle.”

Shalvi Shaksi

3.7 Improve your writing

In this lesson you will…

- write a letter about an important local issue.

1 **Read about the café in Evergreen Park and the letter that appeared in a local newspaper. Why do you think the writer has decided to write to the local newspaper?**

2 **Read the letter again. Answer these questions and support your answers with examples.**

a Is the purpose of the letter clear from the beginning?

b Does the writer consider the advantages and disadvantages of each option?

c What is the writer's opinion?

d Would you agree with the writer if this was happening in your local area?

e Do you think the writer takes a responsible attitude to the issue?

Writing tip

Use **connectives** to link your ideas in writing.

Find examples of each of the following connectives in the letter:

however ***what's more*** ***in addition*** ***as*** ***therefore***

3 **Read about a new shop in the High Street. Write a letter to a local newspaper giving your opinion. Use the letter on the opposite page as a model.**

A new shop in the High Street

Three different businesses are interested in opening a new shop in the High Street.

- The first is a smart designer boutique selling clothes, shoes and accessories.
- The second is a discount store where you can buy the latest fashions at very economical prices.
- The third is a shop staffed by volunteers selling second-hand clothes and household items. You can take things you don't need any more to recycle there.

4
- Have you started each paragraph with a topic sentence?
- Have you included connectives such as *however*, *what's more*, *as* and *therefore*?
- Have you given examples to support your argument?
- Have you addressed the reader directly?

The café in Evergreen Park

The café in your local park has closed. Three people are interested in using it for their own business.

- One wants to make it a top-quality restaurant with international cuisine.
- The second wants to open a fast-food takeaway business serving burgers and pizzas.
- The third wants to turn it into a vegetarian café, run by the community and serving food using locally grown vegetables and fruit.

Start your letter with a sentence or question that engages the reader's attention.

What should happen to the café in Evergreen Park? This is an important issue because the park is the focus of our local area.

There are three options: a top-quality restaurant, a fast-food business and a community café. Each has advantages and disadvantages.

Give a clear idea of the points you're going to cover.

You can start each paragraph with a topic sentence that says what the paragraph is going to be about.

What would a top-quality restaurant bring? It might improve the way people see the local area. People would come to the restaurant and they might spend money in the local shops. However, how many of the local residents could afford to eat there?

However is a useful word, a connective, which introduces a contrasting idea or opinion.

What's more is a connective that introduces additional information.

What's more, a park is where children play. Would they be welcome in a smart restaurant?

A fast-food takeaway might be popular. It's useful when you haven't got time to shop and cook a meal for example. However, as you know, there are several takeaway restaurants in the area already. In addition, a fast-food business would not be good for the local environment as it generates a large amount of waste and litter. Most fast food is sold in plastic or polystyrene packaging, which is often thrown away carelessly. This would quickly become a problem in our park, both for people and for wildlife.

Give examples.

Use personal pronouns to address the reader.

Use the connective *as* (meaning *because*) to introduce an explanation.

The third option, a community café, would have far more advantages than disadvantages. It would provide a place that everyone could use, it would be good for the local economy and it would unite the local community. Therefore, we should definitely support this option.

Give a list of three reasons or examples to support the argument.

Use the connective *therefore* to introduce a conclusion.

3.8 Project challenge

Project 1: A presentation

You are going to give a presentation about an upcycled item.

Do you remember what upcycling is?

1 Work in groups. Ask and answer these questions.

Have you got an idea for something that could be upcycled?

Yes → Draw a diagram or sketch of your idea.

No → Do some research on upcycling. → Find an upcycled item that you like.

Write a description of your item.

It's made from …

You take …

Then you have to …

Next, you …

Finally, …

2 You're going to present your idea to the class. Are you going to …

- give a talk?
- give a digital presentation?
- include photos or drawings?
- bring in an example of your idea to show to the class?

Decide what each person in the group is going to do.

> You're good at drawing. Why don't you draw a diagram or a sketch of our idea?

> Shall we take turns to present our idea?

3 Give your presentation.

4 Ask the class if they have any questions.

5 Ask the class to give their opinions of your presentation.

- How did you decide on an idea for an upcycled item?
- How did working collaboratively help to make your presentation successful?

Project 2: A presentation

You are going to give a presentation about a traditional item of clothing.

1 Work in pairs. Choose a traditional item of clothing.

- **a** What does it look like?
- **b** How do you wear it?
- **c** What is it made of?
- **d** Is there something special about the colours and patterns?
- **e** Where can you buy it?
- **f** Who is it worn by?
- **g** When is it worn?
- **h** How much does it cost?

2 Prepare a short presentation about a traditional item of clothing. Use the steps to help you.

Step 1: Choose an item of clothing to describe.

Step 2: Research the information you need.

Use the questions a–h above as a guide.

Step 3: Decide what sort of presentation you're going to give. Are you going to …

- give a talk to the class?
- give a digital presentation?
- use video?

Step 4: Write your presentation.

Step 5: Find photos or pictures to illustrate your information.

Step 6: Give your presentation.

Step 7: Ask the class if they have any questions.

Step 8: Ask the class to give their opinions of your presentation.

- Did you find the answers to all the questions in Exercise 1, and did you manage to include all the information in your presentation?
- Is there anything you would change in your presentation?

3.9 Poetry

25

1 Read and listen to the poem. What picture do you have in your mind when you read this poem?

Ode to My Shoes

my shoes
rest
all night
under my bed

tired
they stretch
and loosen
their laces

wide open
they fall asleep
and dream
of walking

they revisit
the places
they went to
during the day

and wake up
cheerful
relaxed
so soft

Francisco X. Alarcón

[0] **ode:** a poem written to show you admire someone or something
[6] **stretch:** to straighten your arms, legs or body to full length
[7] **loosen:** to make something less tight
[9] **wide open:** completely open
[18] **cheerful:** happy

Francisco Xavier Alarcón (1954–2016) was born in California and grew up in Mexico. He wrote poems for adults and children, including bilingual poems in Spanish and English.

2 Read and listen to the poem again. Then answer the questions.

a The title of the poem is 'Ode to My Shoes'. Why is this an 'ode'?

b The lines in the poem are very short. What is the effect of this? What kind of feeling does this give the poem? Is it stressful or calm?

c How would the poem be different if the poet had written long lines, like this?
my shoes rest all night under my bed
tired they stretch and loosen their laces

d Look at the word 'tired' in line 5. Is this word usually a negative or positive adjective? How is it used here?

e How and why does the poet use personification in this poem?

3 **Work in small groups. Discuss these questions.**

- **a** Is this a simple or a difficult poem? Give reasons for your answer.
- **b** What do you like about this poem?

26

4 **Read and listen. What picture do you have in your mind when you read this poem?**

Flannel

Red and blue plaid,
pockets with buttons,
my camping shirt
is flannel, worn soft,
pine smells, campfire,
forest moss.

I keep it hidden
in my bottom drawer—
where no one will find it
and wash away
my memories.

Kristine O'Connell George

[1] **plaid:** (pronounced 'plad') cloth with a pattern of different coloured squares and crossed lines

[4] **flannel:** soft cloth made of cotton or wool

[5] **pine:** a tall tree with long, thin leaves shaped like needles

[6] **moss:** a very small, green plant that grows on the surface of rocks, trees, etc.

Kristine O'Connell George (born 1954) writes poetry for children and young people. Her poems often focus on everyday experiences and objects.

5 **Read and listen to the poem again. Then answer the questions.**

- **a** What is the object that the poet is describing?
- **b** Why do you think the title of the poem is 'Flannel' and not the name of the object?
- **c** What do you think the poet likes about the object she's describing?
- **d** How does the poet use the senses in her description?
- **e** What impression do you get of the poet and her interests?
- **f** What does the second verse tell you?

6 **Write a version of this poem in prose. (Prose is ordinary written language, not poetry.) Start like this:**

I've got a red and blue plaid …

7 **Work in pairs. Compare what you wrote in Exercise 6 with the poem.**

8 Read and listen. What picture or pictures do you have in your mind when you read this poem?

A Slash of Blue

A slash of Blue –
A sweep of Gray –
Some scarlet patches on the way,
Compose an Evening Sky –
A little purple – slipped between
Some Ruby Trousers hurried on –
A Wave of Gold –
A Bank of Day –
This just makes out the Morning Sky.

Emily Dickinson

[1] **slash:** a long deep cut made quickly, (*here*) a long thin line
[2] **sweep:** a big curved shape made with a brush
[3] **scarlet:** bright red
[3] **patches:** small pieces of material
[4] **compose:** to come together in order to make (something)
[5] **slipped:** put quickly and quietly in place
[6] **ruby:** deep red
[9] **makes out:** (*here*) enables you to see

Emily Dickinson (1830–1886) is one of America's best-known poets. Her first book of poetry was published in 1890, four years after her death. It was an immediate success. Nature features in many of her poems.

9 Read and listen to the poem again. Then answer the questions.

- a How many colours are mentioned?
- b Which words describe the different shapes of the colours?
- c Do any of the words for shapes surprise you? Why?
- d Does the poem describe an image that stays the same or does it change?
- e How does the poet create a feeling of drama in the poem?

10 Work in pairs. Compare 'A Slash of Blue' with 'Ode to My Shoes' and 'Flannel'. Think about the following:

- the length of the lines
- the choice of words
- the visual images.

11 Write a short poem using one of the three poems you have read as a model. Your poem can be about:

- an item of clothing
- a special possession
- something from the natural world, like the sea, or a forest or a desert.

Check your progress

General knowledge quiz

How much can you remember about what you have learned?

1 Who were the pharaohs?

2 Who wore sandals in Ancient Egypt?

3 What is a hieroglyph?

4 What did these colours symbolise for the Ancient Egyptians?

a Yellow b Green

c White

5 What colour is worn by Chinese women at their wedding, and why?

6 What is the missing word in this sentence?

.... dioxide is a gas that is contributing to climate change.

7 What are **raw materials**? Give two examples.

8 What are **synthetic materials**? Give two examples.

9 Where would you find algae?

10 Give two examples of clothing or footwear that can be made from recycled plastic.

Vocabulary

Clothing and accessories

1 **What are these accessories?**

a You wear them on your ears.

b You wear it around your waist.

c It's a kind of jewellery that you wear on your wrist.

d It's a kind of jewellery that you wear around your neck.

e You wear this on your finger.

f This is made of hair.

g They're usually round and they keep parts of a shirt together.

h You use them to do up your shoes.

2 **Where have all the vowels gone? Complete the words by putting the vowels (*a, e, i, o, u*) in the correct places.**

a p _ l l _ t _ _ n

b r _ c y c l _

c _ n v _ r _ n m _ n t

d c l _ m _ t _

e p l _ s t _ c

f w _ s t _

g r _ b b _ s h

h r _ d _ c _

3 **Choose a word from Exercise 2. Your partner has two chances to guess what the word is. Give your partner clues, but do not say the word.**

Use of English

1 Using multi-word verbs shows that you are really making progress in English. How many of these multi-word verbs can you remember?

When you get dressed, do you always ***put*** your clothes ***on*** in the same order?

- **a** Do you ever forget to *do* .... the laces on your trainers?
- **b** Do you always *try* clothes .... before you buy them?
- **c** Do you like *dressing* .... for special occasions?
- **d** When you *take* your clothes .... at the end of the day, do you *put* them .... carefully?

2 Can you remember how to use modal verbs with the present passive? Look at the example to help you.

You can recycle waste paper.

Waste paper can be recycled.

- **a** We should provide bicycles for people to use in town.
  Bicycles .... for people to use in town.
- **b** You could make your old skateboard into a table!
  Your old skateboard .... into a table!
- **c** You must close the windows when the air-conditioning is on.
  Windows .... when the air-conditioning is on.

Summary checklist

I can

- ☐ describe clothes, parts of clothes, and use multi-word verbs to do with clothes (*put on, do up, try on*).
- ☐ talk about traditional clothes, materials and the significance of clothes.
- ☐ discuss ways of protecting the environment *(must, don't have to, …)*.
- ☐ talk about how waste materials can be reused using the present passive with modals (*shoes can be made from plastic bottles)*.
- ☐ give a short speech about an environmental problem.

4 From A to B

In this unit you will…

- **read** about and discuss transport systems around the world
- **learn** about the history of public transport
- **talk** about how you and people you know travel around
- **use** a variety of adjectives to describe a city (*attractive*, *crowded* …)
- **read** and **talk** about improving the quality of life in cities
- **learn** about how Venice was built and why it is in danger
- **write** a guide to your home town or city.

Getting started

“How many different ways of travelling can you think of?”

Watch this!

4.1 Getting around

In this lesson you will...

- read about and discuss transport systems around the world
- learn vocabulary to talk about transport (*passenger, fare*, ...).

- **What's your favourite way of travelling?**

Vocabulary

1 **Read the text, 'Transport systems around the world', and find the words for the following:**

a someone who travels, but is not the driver of the vehicle ***passenger***
b the price you pay to travel
c a place where you wait for a bus
d too many cars, buses, lorries, etc., making it difficult to move around
e the place where a metro train stops
f someone who regularly travels between home and work
g someone who travels for pleasure
h a ticket that you can use for several train journeys.

Language tip

When you go on a *journey*, you travel from one place to another, usually in a vehicle.

When you go on a *trip*, you go to a place and then come back.

2 **Answer the questions.**

a Why is the bus fare system in Curitiba easy to understand?
b Why is the Curitiba bus system good for the environment?
c What was special about the first metro stations in Moscow?
d Where would you normally expect to find marble columns, mosaics and chandeliers?
e What are the advantages of using the Japanese bullet trains?
f Why might a foreign tourist pay less than a commuter to travel on a Japanese bullet train?

Listening

28

3 **Listen to these adverts for two cities, Copenhagen and Singapore. Which two kinds of transport are mentioned?**

4 **What do these numbers relate to?**

a 375 b 0 c 41 d 3 e 60

5 **Work in pairs. How much can you remember about transport in the two cities?**

Student A, tell Student B about Copenhagen.
Student B, tell Student A about Singapore.

6 **Work in pairs. Write and then record a similar advert for transport in your city.**

TRANSPORT SYSTEMS
AROUND THE WORLD

The buses in Curitiba, a city in southern Brazil, carry half a million passengers a day – that's 30% of the city's population. You buy your ticket before you get on the bus: the fare is the same wherever you're going. No one in the city lives more than 400 metres from a bus stop. Buses are very frequent and the tube-shaped bus shelters are raised to make it easy to get on and off the bus. People don't need to use their cars in the city, so there's less pollution and less congestion on the roads.

The first metro stations in Moscow were built in the 1930s and 1940s as 'palaces for the people'. The architecture was grand and the decoration was elaborate. Komsomolskaya station, for example, has marble columns, mosaics and chandeliers, which you can still see today. The metro carries 7 million passengers a day on weekdays and is known for being frequent and reliable. People say that if you travel by metro in Moscow, you have no excuse for being late.

Japanese bullet trains travel at up to 320 kilometres an hour. The 515 kilometre journey between Tokyo and Osaka, the world's busiest high-speed line, takes around three hours; by car it would take over six. Bullet trains are used by commuters because they're fast, reliable and punctual. They're popular with foreign tourists too, because, as a tourist, you can buy a rail pass that gives you unlimited travel during your trip to Japan.

4.2 By water, rail and road

In this lesson you will...

- learn about the history of public transport
- use the past simple passive to talk about transport.

Key words: Social history

canal
ferry
petrol engine
public transport
the railway age

- **In your country, how did people travel 200 years ago?**

Reading

1 **Look at the words in the social history key words box. Find them in the text. What are they in your language?**

2 **Make a timeline showing a brief history of transport, using the information in the text on the opposite page.**

4000 BCE ***Boats with sails, Mesopotamia*** ***2000 BCE …***

Use of English Past simple passive

We use the past simple passive form when we want to talk about an action, but we don't know who did it, or it's not important to say who did it.

was / were + past participle

The Grand Canal ***was begun*** *in 485 BCE.*

If we want to say who did the action, we use the passive with *by*:

The first buses ***were introduced*** *in France in 1826* ***by*** *Stanislas Baudry.*

In this sentence the action (the introduction of buses) has more importance than the person (Stanislas Baudry), so it comes first.

3 **Make these sentences passive. Use *by* to say who or what did the action.**

a The Ancient Egyptians built boats with a single square sail.
Boats with a single square sail were built by the Ancient Egyptians.

b Horses pulled the buses.

c Karl Benz built the first car in 1885.

d Buses with petrol engines replaced horse-drawn buses.

Writing

4 Write a paragraph about transport in your country.

- *The earliest form of transport was …*
- *It was / They were used to …*
- *Then, in (year), … was / were introduced.*
- *They were powered by …*
- *In (year) … was / were built.*
- *The first (airport / … station) was opened in …*
- *Nowadays, most people travel by …*

A BRIEF HISTORY OF TRANSPORT

A raft made of bamboo

A boat with a sail

The earliest form of public transport was water transport. Boats and rafts made of reeds, wood and animal skins were used as ferries in places as far apart as Egypt and South America. In about 4000 BCE, boats with sails were used in Mesopotamia (now Iraq) and by 2000 BCE, the Egyptians had boats with a single square sail that travelled along the River Nile.

Early Chinese engineers built canals for carrying boats. The Jing-Hang Grand Canal was begun in 485 BCE and completed in 1283, linking Beijing and Hangzhou. Canal locks to enable boats to go from one level to a higher level were first seen in China in 984. The first important canal in Europe was the Canal du Midi in the south of France, completed in 1681.

A canal with a lock

The railway age began in Britain with Richard Trevithick's steam railway locomotive in 1804. The first passenger railway was opened in 1825 in the north of England. At first, people were worried that they wouldn't be able to breathe while travelling so fast – the first trains reached speeds of 25 kilometres per hour!

A steam railway locomotive

The first buses were introduced in France in 1826 by Stanislas Baudry. They were pulled by horses and they were called *voitures omnibus*. Omnibuses first appeared in London in 1829 and could carry 22 passengers. Within a few years, an open upper deck was added to carry more passengers. Road travel changed forever when the first motor car was built by Karl Benz in 1885. Horse-drawn buses disappeared; they were replaced by buses with petrol engines. And, of course, cars began to take over the roads.

An omnibus with an open upper deck

The first car

4.3 Going places

In this lesson you will...

- listen to and summarise an interview with a boy who lives in Morocco
- talk about how you and people you know travel around.

- **What do you like most about travelling? What don't you like?**

Listening

29

1 **Listen to an interview. What aspect of Morocco do we learn about?**

2 **Listen again and complete the notes.**

Malik lives in Casablanca, Morocco

Long-distance trips

Trips to Agadir, the Atlas Mountains and the edge of the Sahara ....[a]

Train journey to Marrakesh

The railway line is ....[b] years old; ....[c] expensive than the bus.

Fares: cheaper tickets for children under ....[d]

Journey time: ....[e] hours, ...[f] minutes

Journey distance: just over ....[g] kilometres

Al Boraq, high-speed train

From Casablanca to Tangier

Speed: ....[h] kph (kilometres per hour)

Features: lower and upper ....[i]

Trip to the Atlas Mountains

By ....[j] to Marrakesh and then by ....[k]

Getting to school

Goes to school by tram

The network was ....[l] in 2012. It was extended in 2019.

3 **Answer these questions.**

a What is Malik's opinion of public transport where he lives?

b Malik says something that surprises the interviewer. What is it?

Speaking and writing tip

Learn a range of phrases for commenting on journeys, trips and holidays. For example, *I really enjoyed it. We had a great time.*

Speaking

4 **Work in pairs. Ask and answer the questions.**

a Is it easy to get around in (name of your country)? Can you give some examples?
It's OK. You can go …

b Are there special fares for young people?
Yes, there are some. For example, …

c Tell me about a journey or a trip you've been on.
Last summer, I went …

d How did you travel?
By …

e How long did the journey take?
The first part of the journey took …

f How far was it?
It was about …

g What was the journey like?
It was great. We saw …

h How do you get around in your day-to-day life? How do you get to school? Do you walk, do you cycle or do you go by car?
Most people …
I usually …

4.4 Two cities

St Petersburg

In this lesson you will...

- use a variety of adjectives to describe a city (*attractive*, *crowded* ...)
- compare cities using *not as* + adjective *as*, *much* (*more*) + adjective ... *than*.

- **What are the advantages and disadvantages of living in a city?**

Vocabulary

1 **Decide which of these adjectives are positive and which are negative when describing a place.**

attractive	congested	friendly	quiet	beautiful	
crowded	historic	noisy	busy	elegant	lively
unattractive	calm	expensive	polluted	unfriendly	

Listening

30

2 **Listen to Lara describing her trip to Russia. Where did she go?**

3 **Discuss these questions. Give reasons for your answers.**

- a Which city do you think she liked best?
- b Which one do you think she would visit again?
- c Which would you prefer to visit, Moscow or St Petersburg?

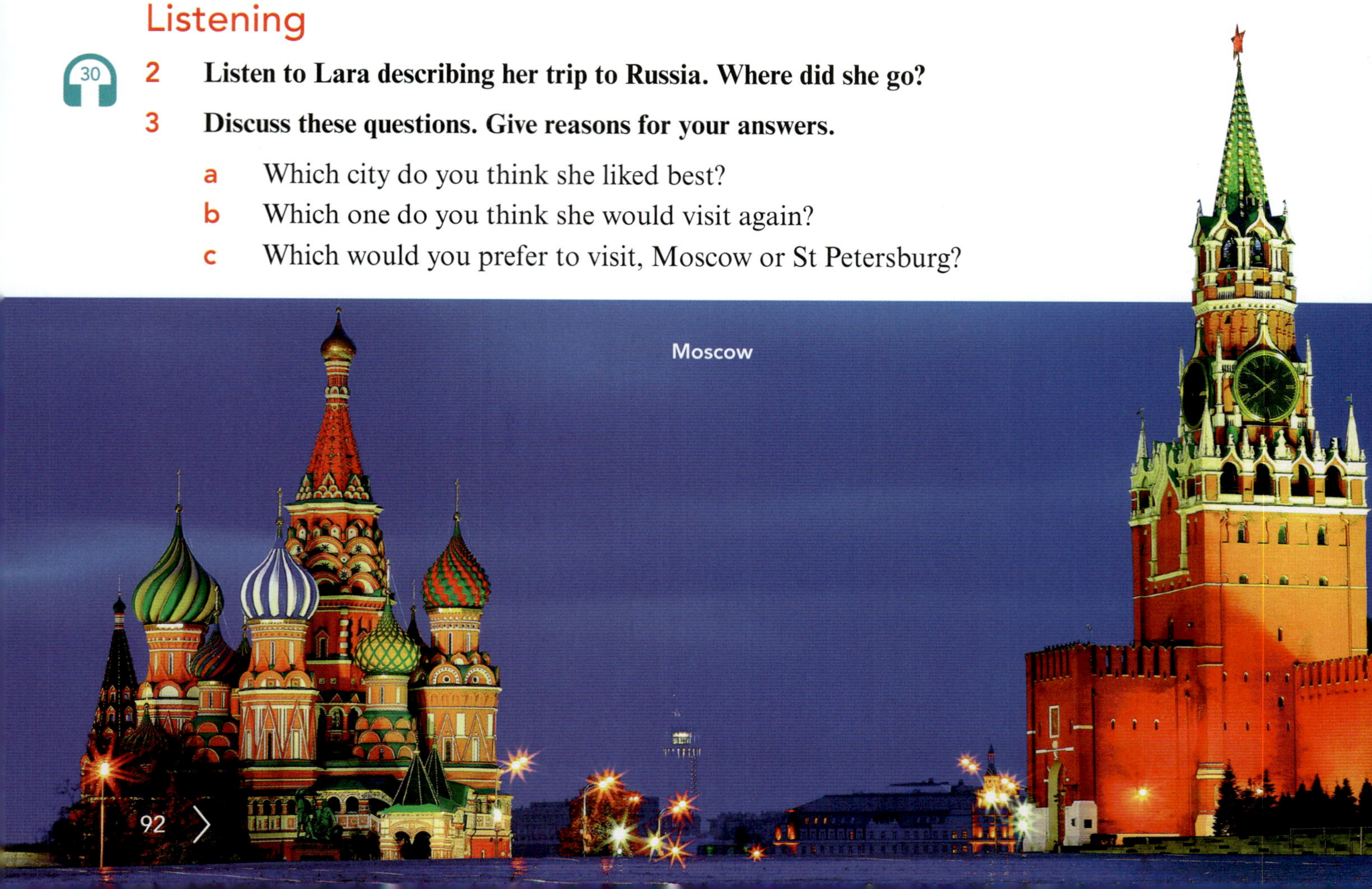
Moscow

Use of English **Comparative adjectives, *not as … as* and *much (more) … than***

- Most one-syllable adjectives make their comparative by adding *-er*: ***calm – calmer***
  Sometimes you have to make spelling changes: ***easy – easier***
- For longer adjectives, including some two-syllable adjectives, use *more* + adjective:
  crowded – more crowded ***attractive – more attractive***
- To make a comparison stronger, use *much*: ***much more polluted***
- Remember to use **than** when comparing two things: St Petersburg is ***quieter than*** *Moscow.*
  Moscow is ***much more polluted than*** *St Petersburg.*
- To make a comparison between things that are or aren't equal, use *(not) as … as*:
  St Petersburg is ***not as busy as*** *Moscow.*

4 **Compare the cities. Complete the chart. Look at the asterisks and examples to help you.**

a	Paris**	Tokyo*	expensive	*Paris is more expensive than Tokyo.*
b	Washington DC*	New York***	small	*Washington DC is much smaller than New York.*
c	Rome*	Athens**	old	*Rome isn't as old as Athens.*
d	Mexico City***	London*	congested	
e	Bangkok**	Jakarta*	hot	
f	Bogotá***	Barranquilla*	high	
g	Ankara*	Istanbul**	big	
h	Florence**	Venice**	beautiful	

Speaking

5 **Work in groups. Discuss and compare towns and cities in your country. Ask and answer using the list of adjectives in Exercise 1.**

A: *Which city do you think is more beautiful, Hanoi or Ho Chi Minh City?*

B: *I think, …*

A: *Why?*

B: *Because …*

4.5 Cities for life

In this lesson you will...

- read and talk about improving the quality of life in cities
- use the comparative form of regular adverbs with (*much*) *more... than*, *not as ... as* and *far less ... than.*

Key words: Science and geography

absorb
evaporation
permeable
reduce
temperature

- **How does a city work? What do people in a city need?**

Reading

1 **Look at the words in the science and geography key words box. Find them in the text and, with a partner, work out their meaning from the context.**

Planning for the FUTURE

By 2050, almost 70% of the world's population will live in cities, so we need to think much more carefully about how we plan them.

You don't usually travel as quickly on a bike as you do in a car. But in some cities today, congestion is so bad that you can get from A to B faster on a bike than in a car. We need to have more cycle paths so that people can cycle more safely. We also need better public transport, so that we use our cars far less frequently than we do now. Some cities, such as Hong Kong, Singapore and Seoul already have excellent public transport systems. The Seoul metro, for example, carries more than 7 million people every day.

We need to be much better at saving water and we need to find ways of using it as efficiently as possible. This includes having 'sponge cities', where rainwater is absorbed and reused. Lingang, which is part of Shanghai, is a 'sponge city'. The city has permeable pavements that – like a sponge – absorb rainwater. This allows evaporation to reduce surface temperature during hot weather. Shanghai also plans to have 400,000 square metres of rooftop gardens with plants, parks and green spaces for rainwater storage.

The Colombian city of Medellín has improved the quality of life for the people who live there. This has been done by planning more creatively than in the past. To bring people together and reduce stress, parks and green spaces were created within the city. In the Parque de los Pies Descalzos (Barefoot Park) for example, people can take off their shoes, walk in sand and massage their feet in a foot spa. Medellín used to be one of the most dangerous cities in the world but now its residents can walk around much more safely and happily than they did 30 years ago.

2 Read the text again and answer the questions.

a Why is it sometimes quicker to cycle than to drive in a city?

b Why does the article mention Hong Kong, Singapore and Seoul?

c What is a 'sponge city'?

d What are two advantages of permeable pavements?

e Why is the park in Medellín called 'Barefoot Park'?

f Is life better in Medellín now? Why?

Use of English
Comparative adverbs, *(much) more … than, not as … as, far less … than*

We usually use *more* to make comparative adverbs.

This has been done by planning ***more creatively than*** *in the past.*

We can use *much* to add emphasis.

We need to think ***much more carefully*** *about how we plan our cities.*

To make negative comparisons, we can use *not as … as* and *far less … than*.

You ***don't*** *usually travel* ***as quickly*** *on a bike* ***as*** *you* ***do*** *in a car.*

… so that we can *use our cars* ***far less frequently than*** *we* ***do*** *now.*

Note that you can use *do* to avoid repetition.

3 Make adverbs from these adjectives. Then use them to complete the sentences.

cheap	frequent	quick

a I can get to school on my bike or by car. On my bike it takes 10 minutes. By car it takes 45 minutes.
I can get to school ***much more quickly on my bike than by car.***

b If you go by bus to Barcelona, the fare is 18 euros. If you go by train, the fare is 65 euros. You can get to Barcelona …………

c You can go by bus or by train. The buses go every 30 minutes. The trains go twice a day. The buses go …………

d You can get from London to Paris by bus in 8 hours. You get there by train in 2 hours 20 minutes. You don't get from London to Paris …………

Speaking

4 Work in groups. Discuss how to improve life in our cities. Choose one aspect (housing, transport, leisure ...). Present your ideas to the class.

We need to (work / plan / think) more (collaboratively / efficiently / creatively) than we do now. For example, …

4.6 Venice: A beautiful city in danger

In this lesson you will...

- learn about how Venice was built and why it is in danger
- talk about Venice by reconstructing what you've heard.

- **Where is Venice? What do you know about it?**

Listening

31

1 Listen to this extract. What is it?

a It's part of an advertising campaign to attract tourists to Venice.

b It's a chapter from a novel or short story.

c It's part of the soundtrack for a TV programme about Venice.

2 Listen again. For each question, choose the correct answer.

a One of the problems Venice has is that

i there aren't as many tourists now as there were in the past.

ii the number of tourists is so much greater than the number of people who live there.

iii people don't want to pay to visit the city.

b Venice is in danger because

i it rains so much that the city is often flooded.

ii there is more pollution in the water.

iii the city is sinking below sea level.

c The best way to get around in Venice is

i to drive.

ii to cycle.

iii to take a boat.

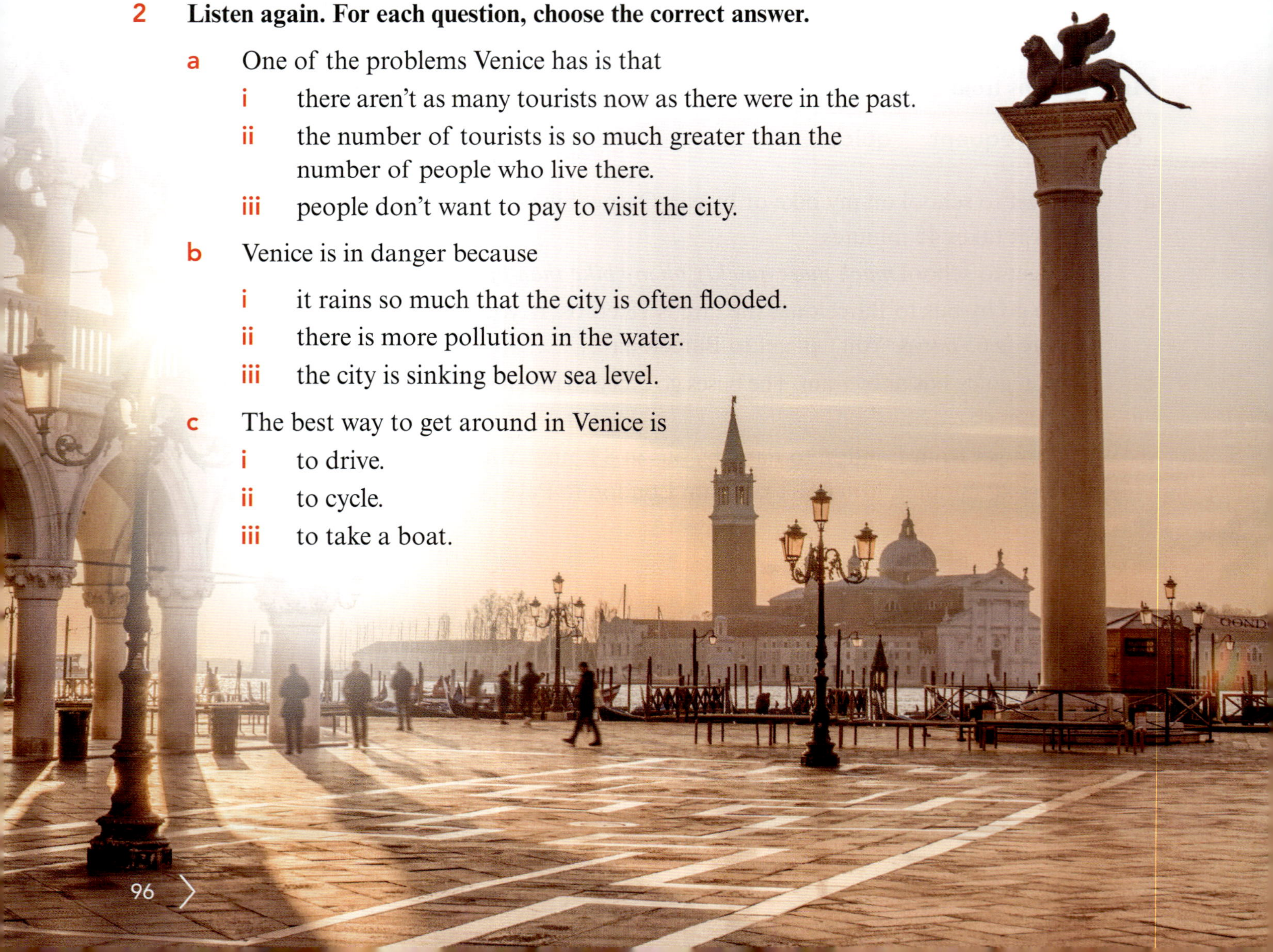

d The houses in Venice were built on wooden platforms
- **i** so that they float on the water like boats.
- **ii** because wood becomes strong in seawater.
- **iii** because wood can easily be replaced.

e There are plans to
- **i** stop tourists visiting Venice.
- **ii** stop too much water coming into the city.
- **iii** stop people travelling on the canals.

Speaking

3 Work in pairs. Take turns to reconstruct what you heard about Venice. Use these notes.

one of the most beautiful cities
25 million visitors a year
small city
50,000 inhabitants
too many tourists
10 euros a day

in danger
sinking by an average of 1 mm to 2 mm per year
climate change causing sea levels to rise
flooded four or five times a year

an unusual city
118 islands
the Adriatic Sea
the north-east coast of Italy

very narrow streets
no cars, motorbikes or motor vehicles
150 canals
public transport: boats called *vaporetti*
travel in style: gondola

trip, Grand Canal
houses and palaces
wooden platforms
wood under water, not in contact with oxygen
in saltwater, as hard as stone

several projects: flood barriers (gates)
control water
control number of tourists
plan trips carefully

4.7 Improve your writing

In this lesson you will...

- write a guide to your home town or city.

You're going to write a guide to your home town or city for a visitor.

1 Read the text. Choose a heading for each section.

Places to go, things to see	The background story
Looking to the future	Getting around

2 Avoid repetition by varying the verbs you use. How does the writer avoid using the verb *go* in each of the following sentences?

a You can get there by boat.

b You can visit some of the three hundred temples in the city.

c Climb up inside the temple to get a wonderful view from the top.

d You should certainly experience the colourful floating markets in Bangkok.

3 Find six adjectives that add colour and interest to the description.

4 Write a guide to your town or city for a visitor. Use the description of Bangkok as a model.

- Have you used the present passive and past passive?
- Have you used relative clauses to give extra information?
- Have you used a variety of adjectives?
- Have you used sentence adverbs such as *certainly*, *fortunately* and *unfortunately*?
- Have you used a variety of verbs to avoid repetition?

Remember to use the past passive when you want to focus on what was done rather than who did it.

The present passive is similarly useful to describe current situations.

Use non-defining relative clauses to give extra information.

Use a variety of adjectives, including compound adjectives, to add colour and interest to your descriptions.

Use sentence adverbs, such as *certainly, fortunately, unfortunately,* to show what your opinion is.

Address the readers directly, to make them feel involved.

My city, Bangkok

a …………

Bangkok became the capital of Siam, now Thailand, in 1782. The city was built on the banks of the Chao Praya river. A network of canals was also developed, and for this reason Bangkok was known as 'the Venice of the East'. The canals are still used today by thousands of commuters and also by tourists.

b …………

The Grand Palace, which is on the east bank of the river, was the home of the Thai kings. You can get there by boat. It's a spectacular building and the city's best-known landmark. It's also home to the Emerald Buddha.

You can visit some of the three hundred temples in the city. Don't miss the Temple of Dawn, which is particularly beautiful at sunrise and sunset. Climb up inside the temple to get a wonderful view from the top.

You should certainly experience the colourful floating markets in Bangkok, where you can buy fresh fruit and vegetables and you can also eat delicious, freshly cooked, homemade food.

c …………

In addition to exploring the historic and cultural attractions on the riverside by river taxis and boats, you can also get to the main shopping and business areas using the Skytrain, an elevated train system, and the underground metro network.

d …………

Unfortunately, Bangkok and Venice have something else in common. Ocean levels are rising and the city is sinking by 1 to 2 centimetres a year, so it's actually sinking more quickly than Venice. There is a huge risk of flooding in the near future. The government is building new canals to control the water and the university has built a large park to absorb rainwater and redirect it, so that other areas are not flooded.

4.8 Project challenge

Project 1: Unusual ways of getting to school

You're going to write a text for the webpage 'Unusual ways of getting to school'.

In Cambodia, there are two seasons, wet and dry. During the wet season, which lasts from May to October, heavy rainfall means that rivers flood into surrounding areas. Getting to school by road becomes difficult and dangerous for many children. Village leaders and parents in Battambang province hire a boat to take the children to school along the river. This means that children can get to school much more easily and much more safely. They don't have to miss lessons for six months of the year.

Step 1: Work in small groups. Look up information about unusual ways of getting to school.

Step 2: How many examples did you find? Decide which one you're going to write about.

Step 3: Write a draft of your text. Use the one about Cambodia as a model.

- Give some information about the country or region.
- Say why the journey to school is difficult.
- Describe how children get to school.
- Give any advantages or disadvantages of the way they travel.
- Compare the way the children travel with your own journey to school.
- Find a photo to illustrate your text.

Step 4: Read your text carefully. Check the spelling and punctuation.

Step 5: Write your final version.

- What did you learn from looking up information for this project?
- How did you use the model text?
- What did you learn from doing this project?

Project 2: Six reasons to live in my town / city

You're going to give a slide presentation of six reasons to live in your town or city.

Step 1: Work in small groups. Read the outline of the presentation about Helsinki below.

Step 2: Share your opinions about why your home town is a good place to live. Decide on the six best reasons to live in your town or city.

Step 3: Write the titles and the text for each slide. If possible, find a picture for each one.

Step 4: Decide who is going to present each slide. Give your presentation.

1 Not too big, not too small

Helsinki is not too big and not too small and you can get out into the countryside easily.

2 Leisure and social life

There are swimming pools, sports fields and running paths. There are youth centres where you can spend your free time playing games and doing music, dance and drama classes. You can also go on day trips and on camps.

3 I don't speak Finnish!

Helsinki is a great place for those who don't speak Finnish. Most people understand English because everyone learns it at school.

4 Education

Schools are good and they are free. The standard of education is one of the highest in the world. Schools believe that competition isn't as important as cooperation.

5 Transport

You can go everywhere by bike. There is a 1200-kilometre network of cycle paths. You can rent a bike or use city bikes. There are buses and trams, there's a metro and there are local railway and ferry services.

6 Green spaces

More than a third of the city's area is given over to green spaces, such as parks and gardens.

- What are the advantages of working in a group for this type of project?
- www – What went well?
- ebi – Even better if …

4.9 Song lyrics

'Big Yellow Taxi' was written and recorded by the Canadian singer-songwriter Joni Mitchell in 1970. This is how she described the inspiration for the song:

> 'I wrote "Big Yellow Taxi" on my first trip to Hawaii. I took a taxi to the hotel and when I woke up the next morning, I threw back the curtains and saw these beautiful green mountains in the distance. Then, I looked down and there was a parking lot as far as the eye could see, and it broke my heart... this blight* on paradise. That's when I sat down and wrote the song.'

* A **blight** is a serious disease that attacks plants and crops. It can also be used to mean something ugly or bad that is spoiling something beautiful.

1 **Read the lyrics and listen to the song online. It was popular when it came out and it is still popular today. Why do you think this is?**

2 **Answer these questions about the language of the song.**

- a How would you say, '*Don't* it always seem to go …?' in Standard English?
- b What is the usual way of writing, and saying, 'put *'em* in a tree museum'?
- c Look at the ends of the lines. Which words rhyme? Are there any half-rhymes (words that almost rhyme)?
- d Songs often have verses and a chorus. The verses are different from one another, the chorus stays the same. Which are the verses in this song? Which is the chorus?
- e At the end of the song, why do you think Joni Mitchell repeats the lines *They paved paradise / And put up a parking lot*?

3 **Answer these questions about the meaning and purpose of the song.**

- a Does the song have a message? If so, what is it?
- b Why do you think Joni Mitchell wrote this song?
- c What is the difference between writing a pop song about this topic and writing an essay or an article in a magazine?

Big Yellow Taxi

They paved paradise
And put up a parking lot
With a pink hotel, a boutique
And a swinging hot spot

Don't it always seem to go
That you don't know what you've got till it's gone
They paved paradise
And put up a parking lot

They took all the trees
And put 'em in a tree museum
And they charged the people
A dollar and a half just to see 'em

Don't it always seem to go,
That you don't know what you've got till it's gone
They paved paradise
And put up a parking lot

Hey farmer farmer
Put away that DDT now
Give me spots on my apples
But leave me the birds and the bees
Please!

Don't it always seem to go
That you don't know what you've got till it's gone
They paved paradise
And put up a parking lot

Late last night
I heard the screen door slam
And a big yellow taxi
Took away my old man

Don't it always seem to go
That you don't know what you've got till it's gone
They paved paradise
And put up a parking lot

They paved paradise
And put up a parking lot

[2] **parking lot:** (American English) car park

[3] **boutique:** a small fashionable shop, usually selling clothes

[4] **swinging hot spot:** a popular disco or club

[7] **paved:** put a hard, flat surface on an area of ground

[27] **screen door:** (American English) a door with wire or plastic net in it, to let air in and keep insects out

Notes

- The Royal Hawaiian Hotel, Waikiki, Hawaii, is thought to be the 'pink hotel' described in the song.
- The 'tree museum' is thought to be the Foster Botanical Garden in Honolulu, where you pay to see trees and plants.
- In the 1940s and 1950s, farmers began using DDT to protect their crops from insects. It is no longer used in most countries because it is an environmental poison, affecting not only insects, but birds, fish and humans. It was still used in the USA in 1970, when Joni Mitchell wrote this song.
- Joni Mitchell doesn't say why the big yellow taxi has come to take away her old man (which can mean her partner or father). She leaves us to guess.

4 **Read the lyrics and listen to this song by The Pretenders by searching online. The Pretenders are an English-American rock band. The lead singer, Chrissie Hynde, is from Akron, Ohio in the USA.**

'My City Was Gone'

I went back to Ohio
But my city was gone
There was no train station
There was no downtown
South Howard had disappeared
All my favourite places
My city had been pulled down
Reduced to parking spaces
Ay, oh, way to go, Ohio

Well, I went back to Ohio
But my family was gone
I stood on the back porch
There was nobody home
I was stunned and amazed
My childhood memories
Slowly swirled past
Like the wind through the trees
Ay, oh, way to go, Ohio

I went back to Ohio
But my pretty countryside
Had been paved down the middle
By a government that had no pride
The farms of Ohio
Had been replaced by shopping malls
And Muzak filled the air
From Seneca to Cuyahoga Falls
Said, ay, oh, way to go, Ohio

5 **Work in small groups. Compare this song with 'Big Yellow Taxi'.**

Think of the following:

- the mood of the song
- the tempo (Quick? Slow?)
- the structure (verses, choruses, rhymes)
- lines and words that are repeated
- the message of the song.

Language tip

Try to use comparative adjectives in your discussion:

not as … as …

much (slower / more upbeat) … than …

6 **Work in small groups. You are going to write a song about a topic that is important to you (it can be an environmental issue, or it can be something different).**

a Discuss your ideas for a topic.

b One member of the group should summarise the ideas and help the group to reach a decision about which idea or ideas would make a good song. (You may be able to combine ideas.)

c Decide on the mood and the tempo of the song.

d Decide on the structure of the song (verses, choruses, rhymes).

e Write the song. Try singing the lines as you write them.

Check your progress

General knowledge quiz

How much can you remember about what you have learned?

1 They were built almost a hundred years ago and they were known as 'palaces of the people'. No one lives there, but they are used by millions of people every day. What are they?

2 What is a 'bullet train'?

3 Which city was voted 'the world's best cycle city'?

4 Why are canals built with locks?

5 What is this?

6 When did Karl Benz build the first car? Was it 1835, 1885 or 1935?

7 What do we call 'omnibuses' today?

8 This city has canals, a metro system, a Winter Palace and it's in Russia. What is it called?

9 Venice is made up of a group of islands in which sea: the North Sea, the Aegean, or the Adriatic?

10 Why is the Italian city of Venice in danger?

Vocabulary

Transport

1 **Choose the correct word.**

a Bullet trains can reach 320 kilometres *one* / ***an*** hour.

b You can catch the bus at the bus *stop* / *place* over there.

c How much is the bus *cost* / *fare*?

d My Russian friend goes to school *by* / *on* metro.

e The metro is the best way for *commuters* / *tourists* to get to work.

f How long did the journey *make* / *take*?

2 **Match the words to the definitions.**

passenger fare shelter congestion commuter tourist pass

a the price you pay to travel

b a place where you wait for a bus

c someone who regularly travels between home and work

d someone who travels for pleasure

e too many cars, buses, lorries, etc., making it difficult to move around

f a ticket that you can use for several journeys

g someone who travels, but is not the driver of the vehicle

Use of English

1 Complete the text by changing the verbs in brackets into the past simple passive.

The early history of the bicycle

The bicycle ***was invented***[a] *(invent)* by the German Karl von Drais in 1817. It had two wheels, but no pedals. You pushed it along with your feet. It ....[b] *(know)* as the 'draisine' after its inventor and it ....[c] *(make)* of wood. The word 'bicycle' appeared in the 1860s when it ....[d] *(use)* to replace the French name *vélocipède à pédales*.

Pedals ....[e] *(add)* to the front wheel of the bicycle in 1864. The first inflatable rubber tyres for a bicycle ....[f] *(invent)* by a Scottish man called John Dunlop in 1888.

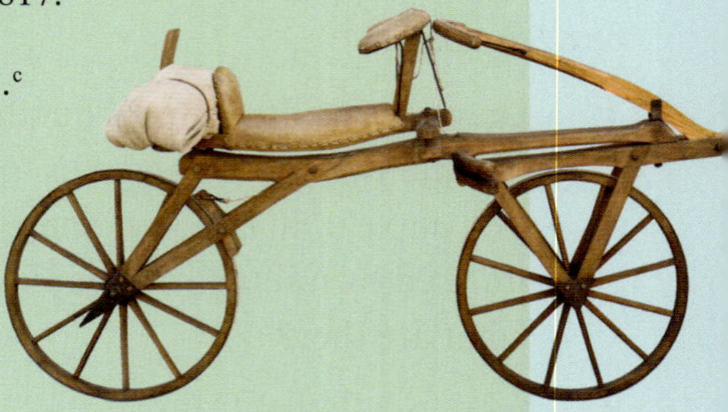

2 Make adverbs and comparative adverbs from these adjectives. Then use them to complete the sentences below.

adjective	safe	cheap	careful	quick	easy
adverb	***safely***				
comparative	***more safely***				

a You can ride around the city ***much more safely*** if you use the cycle paths. (use *much*)

b The bus fare is 2 euros, but the train fare is 10 euros. So you can travel .... by bus. (use *much*)

c The bus takes an hour to get into town, whereas the metro only takes ten minutes. So you don't get there .... by bus .... you do by metro. (use *as*)

d I was going much too fast on my bike and I fell off. I cycle .... now. (use *much*)

e You have to change trains four times to get from the city to my village. The bus, however, takes you straight there. You get there .... by train. (use *far less*)

Summary checklist

I can

☐ talk about transport systems around the world.
☐ write and record an advert for transport in my city.
☐ read and understand a text about the history of transport.
☐ talk about travelling around in my country.
☐ compare towns and cities and discuss ways of improving quality of life in cities.
☐ understand someone talking about Venice and reconstruct what I've heard.

5 The great outdoors

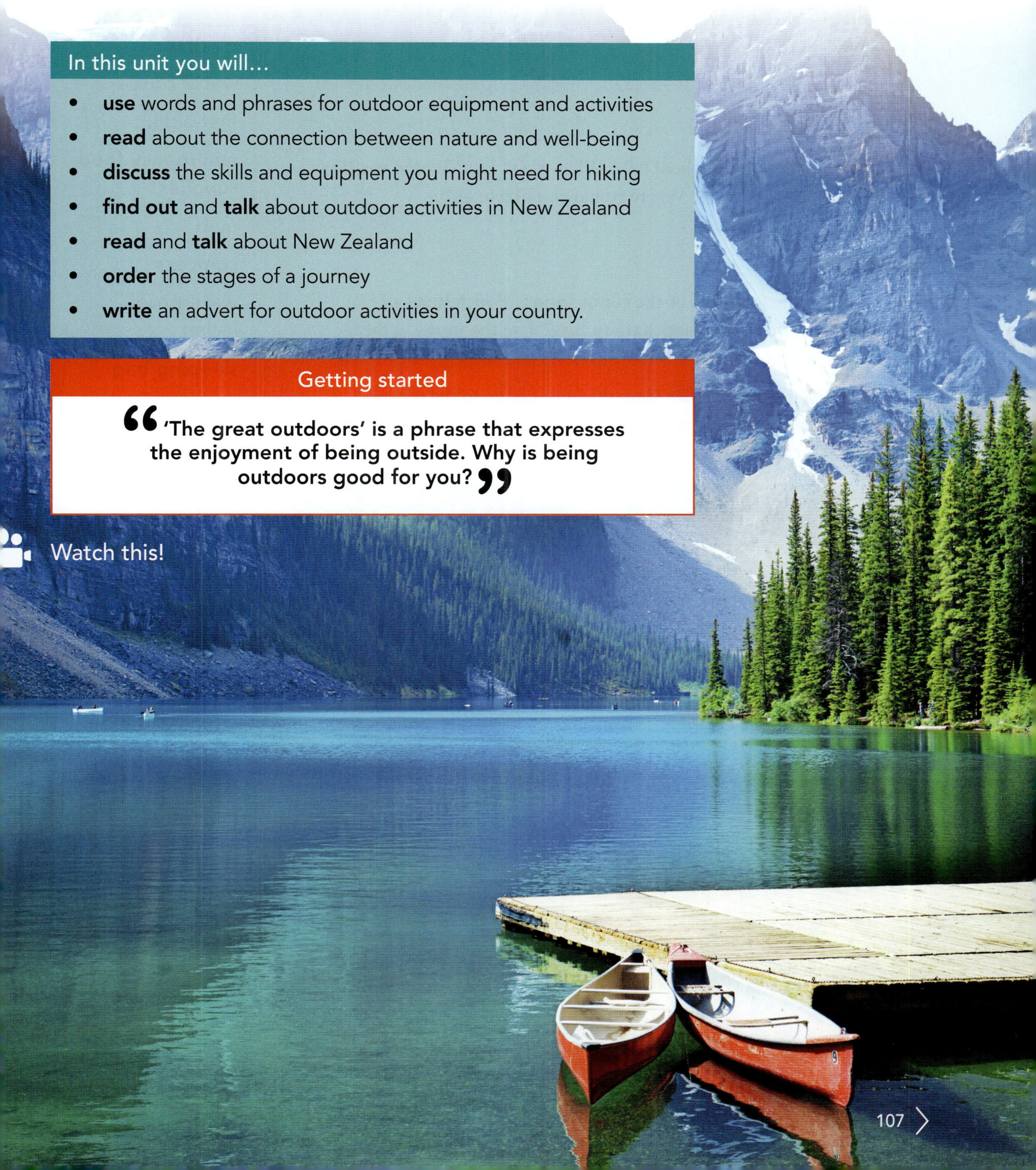

In this unit you will...

- **use** words and phrases for outdoor equipment and activities
- **read** about the connection between nature and well-being
- **discuss** the skills and equipment you might need for hiking
- **find out** and **talk** about outdoor activities in New Zealand
- **read** and **talk** about New Zealand
- **order** the stages of a journey
- **write** an advert for outdoor activities in your country.

Getting started

“'The great outdoors' is a phrase that expresses the enjoyment of being outside. Why is being outdoors good for you?”

Watch this!

5.1 A school trip

In this lesson you will...

- use words and phrases for outdoor equipment and activities
- talk about going on a school trip using *-ing* forms (*putting up a tent is easy, …*).

- **Have you been on a school trip? What was it like? Would you like to go on a school trip? Where would you like to go?**

Listening

32 **1** **Listen to the first part of the conversation. Which items of equipment do the students have to take? Use the words in the box to help you.**

33 **2** **Copy the list of activities from the box. Listen to the second part of the conversation. Number the activities in the order they're mentioned.**

Equipment

water bottle
first-aid kit
emergency food supplies
map
compass
waterproof jacket
sleeping bag
torch

Outdoor activities

make a campfire
cook over a campfire
put up a tent
follow a path
identify trees, plants and wildlife
find your way
read a map
use a compass

Use of English *-ing* forms

We use *-ing* forms (verb + *-ing*) in English where some other languages use infinitives.

Look at the examples. How would you say these sentences in your language?

-ing forms as subjects: ***Putting** up a tent is easy.*

-ing forms as objects: *I like **looking** at maps.*

-ing forms after a preposition: *I'm no good at **putting** up a tent.*

Speaking

34 **3** **Work in pairs. Imagine you're going on a school trip. Ask and answer these questions. You can listen to a model conversation to help you.**

a **A:** Are you good at reading a map?
B: ***Well, I don't know. I've never tried. What about you?***
A: ***Yes, I like maps and I like trying to find my way with one. But using a compass isn't easy.***

b Are you good at putting up a tent?

c Do you like sleeping in a tent?

d What about cooking over a campfire? What's that like?

e Are you interested in identifying plants and animals?

5.2 The power of nature

In this lesson you will...

- read about the connection between nature and well-being
- discuss and evaluate a theory about the benefits of spending time in the outdoors.

Key words: Health education

energy
stress
to refresh
to relax
vitality
worry

- **You are going to read an extract from a book called *Forest Bathing*. What do you think the book is about?**

Reading

1 **Before you read, look up the words in the health education key words box in a dictionary. Then answer these questions.**

a What can cause stress and worry?

b What can give you energy and vitality?

c How do you relax?

d What refreshes you when you're tired?

2 **Read the text. What do we know about the writer?**

3 **Answer the questions.**

a What is *shinrin-yoku*?

b According to the writer, what are the sounds you should listen for in a forest?

c How can you use your sense of touch in a forest?

d Why do you think the author says 'this is not exercise, or hiking, or jogging'?

e What is the purpose of the last paragraph?

f The book *Forest Bathing* is written mainly for adults. How do you think the author's ideas might be useful for people your age?

We all know how good being in nature can make us feel. We have known it for centuries. The sounds of the forest, the scent of the trees, the sunlight playing through the leaves, the fresh, clean air – these things give us a sense of comfort. They ease our stress and worry, help us to relax and to think more clearly. Being in nature can restore our mood, give us back our energy and vitality, refresh and rejuvenate us.

But what exactly is this feeling that is so hard to put into words? I am a scientist, not a poet. And I have been investigating the science behind that feeling for many years.

[2] **scent:** a nice smell

[3] **ease:** to become less bad

[5] **restore:** to make something good exist again

[6] **rejuvenate:** to make something or someone young again

[8] **investigate:** to try to get all the facts about something

In Japan, we practise something called forest bathing, or *shinrin-yoku*. *Shinrin* in Japanese means 'forest', and *yoku* means 'bath'. So *shinrin-yoku* means bathing in the forest atmosphere, or taking in the forest through our senses. This is not exercise, or hiking, or jogging. It is simply being in nature, connecting with it through our senses of sight, hearing, taste, smell and touch. *Shinrin-yoku* is like a bridge. By opening our senses, it bridges the gap between us and the natural world.

***

The key to unlocking the power of the forest is in the five senses. Let nature enter through your ears, eyes, nose, mouth, hands and feet. Listen to the birds singing and the breeze rustling in the leaves of the trees. Look at the different greens of the trees and the sunlight filtering through the branches. Smell the fragrance of the forest. … Taste the freshness of the air as you take deep breaths. Place your hands on the trunk of a tree. Dip your fingers or toes in a stream. Lie on the ground. Drink in the flavour of the forest and release your sense of joy and calm. This is your sixth sense, a state of mind. Now you have connected with nature. You have crossed the bridge to happiness.

***

You can forest-bathe anywhere in the world – wherever there are trees; in hot weather or in cold; in rain, sunshine or snow. You don't even need a forest. Once you have learned how to do it, you can do *shinrin-yoku* anywhere – in a nearby park or in your garden. Look for a place where there are trees, and off you go!

[15] **bridge the gap:** to reduce the differences or distances between two things

[19] **rustling:** the noise made by leaves in the wind

[20] **filtering:** if light or sound filters into a place, only a little of it comes in

[21] **fragrance:** a nice smell

[23] **dip:** to move (something) down for a short time

[24] **release:** to allow something to be free

[25] **joy:** a strong feeling of happiness

[25] **state of mind:** how you are feeling at a particular time

Speaking

4 You are going to work in two groups, A and B, for the following role-play exercise.

Group A You don't believe in *shinrin-yoku*. Give your reasons.

It all sounds a bit too good to be true.

It's much better for you to go out and play football or do something really energetic.

What about if you don't live near a forest?

How do you know it works?

I'd feel really silly touching trees and dipping my toes in the water.

Group B You have to persuade the students in Group A to change their minds.

Here are some idiomatic phrases that might be useful.

there's no harm in trying	*you might change your mind*
you've got nothing to lose	*it makes sense*
as a matter of fact	*take advantage of*

> 5.3 Finding your way

In this lesson you will...

- discuss the skills and equipment you might need for hiking
- role-play a conversation in which you have to work out what to do in a difficult situation.

- **Hiking is going for a long walk in the countryside. Why do you think people go hiking?**

Reading

1 **Read the advert for the Outdoor Centre. Who would go there, and why?**

The Outdoor Centre

Navigation skills

Follow marked paths and tracks in a national park using a map and a compass.

First aid

It's important to know basic first aid so that you can deal with an emergency.

Camping skills

Learn how to put up a tent and how to build a shelter using materials that you find nearby, such as wood, rocks and branches.

2 **Work in groups. Discuss these questions.**

a When might you need to use a map and a compass?

b When might a first-aid kit be useful?

c When might you need to build a shelter?

3 **Read this scenario. Then answer the question: How do you decide what to do?**

> **Today is the first day of your activity holiday. The instructor describes this situation.**
> 'You're walking with your friends in a mountainous area. You've walked 15 kilometres and now it's getting dark. You're following a path but you're not sure where it goes. You think your destination is about 5 kilometres away. You haven't got a tent. You've only got emergency food rations. You've each got a full bottle of water. Do you continue? Do you go back? Do you decide to build a shelter and carry on when it gets light in the morning? How do you decide what to do?'

35

4 **Listen to a phone conversation. What's the problem?**

5 **Listen again. Then answer the questions.**

a Where is the woman who answers the phone?

b Who is making the phone call?

c Why is he phoning?

d Where are the boys?

e What information does the woman try to find out?

f What information does the boy give?

g What does the woman suggest?

> **Remember**
>
> **Present simple and present continuous**
>
> *You **learn** useful skills at an outdoor activity centre.*
>
> *Today we**'re learning** navigation skills.*
>
> We often use present tenses to describe imaginary situations.
>
> *You**'re walking** with your friends in a mountainous area.*
> *It**'s getting** dark.*
>
> ***Do** you **continue**? **Do** you **go back**?*

Speaking

6 **Work in pairs. Role-play the dialogue you've just heard. Use the information from your answers to Exercise 5.**

7 **Now role-play this situation. One of you is making the call. The other answers the phone at the Outdoor Centre.**

> You're walking in the mountains. There's a strong wind and you've lost your map because the wind blew it away. You don't know where you are but you think you're about 10 kilometres from the Outdoor Centre. You're following a path and you're walking towards a small lake ahead of you in the valley. There are trees and bushes near the lake. The sun is low in the sky behind you. It's getting dark. Phone the Outdoor Centre for advice.

5.4 The land of adventure

In this lesson you will...

- find out and talk about outdoor activities in New Zealand
- ask and answer questions about doing particular outdoor activities.

- **Where is New Zealand? What do you know about it?**

Vocabulary

1 **Read the information about outdoor activities in New Zealand. List the activities under three headings. (Some can come under more than one heading.) Leave out any you don't know.**

Land	Air	Water
snowboarding	***skydiving***	***fishing***

Speaking and writing tip

Learning words in groups can help you to remember them.

From hiking to skydiving, New Zealand has it all

Are you interested in seeing new places? Do you dream of going on an activity holiday? Are you keen on trying new things? Then New Zealand is the place for you.

Start in Queenstown, known as the 'Adventure Capital of the World' because it offers every outdoor activity you can think of doing. You might enjoy hiking in the hills and mountains. You may want to spend time fishing or sailing. Perhaps you feel like doing something more energetic, such as kayaking, skiing, snowboarding or mountain biking. Do you fancy trying an extreme sport like bungee jumping or canyoning? If you're really adventurous, perhaps skydiving is for you!

How about swimming with dolphins? Well, think of going to Akaroa Harbour, where you can swim with the world's smallest dolphins. At the end of the day, you can look forward to exploring the Te Anau Glow-worm Caves, where you will see underground waterfalls and more. Imagine visiting a dark area of the caves where thousands of glow-worms light up the space!

SAFETY FIRST

- YOUR SAFETY IS OUR BUSINESS.
- ALL ACTIVITIES ARE ORGANISED BY QUALIFIED INSTRUCTORS.
- FOR SOME ACTIVITIES, CHILDREN MUST BE ACCOMPANIED BY AN ADULT.

2 Discuss these questions.

a Where might you read the text in Exercise 1?

b Who is it aimed at and what does it aim to do?

c What effect does it have on you?

Listening

36 **3 Listen to Alana telling her mum about New Zealand. What is Alana's attitude to outdoor pursuits and what does her mum think about them?**

4 Listen again. What are these outdoor pursuits? If necessary, add them to your lists in Exercise 1.

a bungee jumping
b paragliding
c zorbing
d white-water rafting
e canyoning

Speaking

5 Test your partner. Take it in turns to choose an activity from the lists in Exercise 1. Describe the activity without naming it. Your partner has to say what it is.

A: *It's a winter sport and you do it on snow. It's a bit like skiing.*

B: *Is it snowboarding?*

A: *Yes, it is. OK, your turn.*

6 Write five questions using the words in the table. Then ask and answer them with a partner.

Are you interested in doing a bungee jump?

Can you imagine	do	a bungee jump / a parachute jump?
Are you interested in		
What about	swim	with dolphins?
Would you be good at	explore	an underground cave?
Have you ever dreamed of		

7 How would you feel about doing these activities? Write sentences that are true for you.

Swimming with dolphins	sounds	fun
Bungee jumping	could be	terrifying
Zorbing	might be	dangerous
Seeing the glow-worms		interesting

5.5 The land of the long white cloud

In this lesson you will...

- read and talk about New Zealand
- write a fact file about Australia.

Key words: Geography

capital
glacier
island
landscape
population
province
volcano

- **How would you describe the landscape of your country?**

Reading

1 **Read about New Zealand on the opposite page. Which two topics are *not* included in the text?**

- history
- geography
- climate
- sport
- customs and traditions
- animals
- transport

2 **Find these words in the text. Try to work out their meaning from the context.**

a inhabited
b cartographer
c anglicised
d flightless
e species

3 **Write one or two questions to ask about the information in each paragraph.**

How many islands are there in New Zealand?

4 **Take it in turns to ask your questions. The other students in the class must answer without looking at the text.**

Remember Superlatives

Add -*est* to adjectives to make superlatives: *small – smallest*

There are spelling changes for some superlatives: *dry – driest, flat – flattest.*

Find three superlative adjectives in the text.

Writing

5 **Use the fact file about Australia to make an information display, similar to the one about New Zealand. Find photos to illustrate it.**

Australia is the world's oldest, driest and flattest continent. …

New Zealand is made up of two main islands, the North Island and the South Island, and about six hundred smaller ones. It was the last area on Earth to be inhabited by humans. It is thought that over eight hundred years ago, people from islands in the Pacific Ocean travelled thousands of miles in small canoes to reach New Zealand. They were the ancestors of the Māori people. They named their country Aotearoa, meaning 'land of the long white cloud'.

New Zealand's landscape includes mountains, glaciers, lakes, rivers, forests and volcanoes. The South Island is more mountainous than the North Island: two-thirds of the island is made up of mountains, which include the Southern Alps and New Zealand's longest glacier, the Tasman Glacier.

In 1642, the Dutch explorer, Abel Tasman, arrived. Three years later, Dutch cartographers made maps of the country and called it 'Nova Zeelandia', after the Dutch province of Zeeland. The name was anglicised by the British explorer James Cook in 1769, and so it became 'New Zealand'.

New Zealand was the first country to give women the right to vote, in 1893. The government is based in the capital, Wellington, in the North Island.

There are just under 5 million New Zealanders, who are informally known as 'Kiwis'. A kiwi is a brown flightless bird that is only found in New Zealand, along with many other species unique to the country. These include the kakapo, the world's heaviest parrot, which, like the kiwi, doesn't fly, and Hector's dolphins, the smallest dolphins in the world.

Rugby is the national sport of New Zealand. The country's team is called the 'All Blacks' and is one of the best teams in the world. The players are famous for their pre-match haka, which is based on a traditional Māori war dance.

FACT FILE

Australia: the world's oldest, driest, flattest continent

First inhabitants: the Aboriginal people, who arrived by sea from Asia more than 60,000 years ago. Population now over 24 million.

Name: from Latin *australis* meaning 'southern'.

Landscape: vast areas of desert; tropical rainforests and coral reefs in the north-east; mountains in the east of country; 18,000 kilometres of coast; woods in island Tasmania.

1616 Dutch explorer Dirk Hartog arrived.

1642–44 Abel Tasman explored, cartographers made maps.

1770 Captain Cook established British settlements, English became the main language.

Women given the vote in 1902.

Government: based in Canberra (capital city).

Unique species: kangaroo, koala bear, platypus.

Most popular sports: cricket, rugby league, Australian-rules football, netball.

5.6 Alana goes to New Zealand

In this lesson you will...

- put the stages of a journey into the correct order
- talk about future plans.

- **How would you travel to New Zealand from your country? How long would it take?**

Reading

1 **Look at the following messages. Answer the questions.**

a Who is going on a journey? Who is she going to visit?

b Put the messages **a–j** in chronological order.

Alana

a What shall I bring with me? What's the weather going to be like? Am I going to need wet-weather gear? I want to go kayaking and white-water rafting. Do I need to bring a helmet and a life jacket?

b I'm just waiting for my bag to come through. See you in a minute.

c I've packed my bag, I've checked in online and I've got my boarding pass, so I'm all set.

d

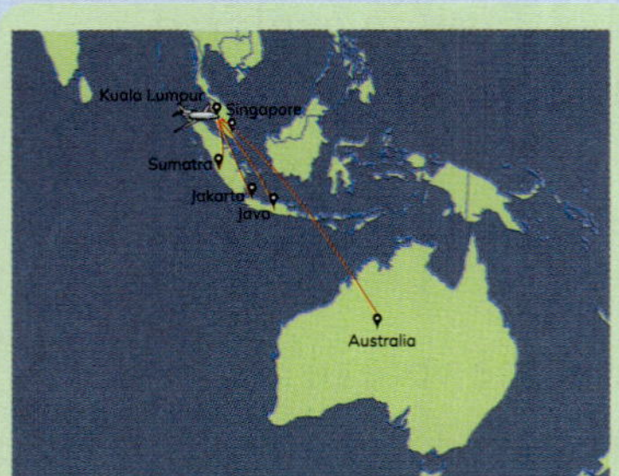

Not far to go now!

e Hi, Auntie Paula. I'm coming to see you in December. Mum's just booked the ticket. I leave on the 21st and I arrive on the 23rd. I can't wait! Love, Alana.

f Thanks, Auntie Paula. I haven't got a wetsuit but we're going to get one tomorrow.

g **Paula**

You won't need any special equipment. It's all provided at the Activity Centre. And you won't need waterproof stuff – we've got lots here and in any case, it'll be warm and dry. But bring a wetsuit if you've got one. You'll enjoy surfing at Whale Bay!

h Hi Alana. I'm really pleased that you're coming. We'll have a great time!

i I'm leaving for the airport now and I'll wait for you in the coffee bar near the exit. See you soon.

j See you tomorrow! Have a good flight.

Listening

37 **2 Listen and check. Then answer these questions.**

- a When is Alana going to New Zealand?
- b Which outdoor pursuits does she want to try?
- c What will she need when she goes surfing?
- d What's the weather going to be like?
- e Where will Paula meet Alana?

Use of English Expressing the future

Present continuous

- For fixed arrangements future: *I'**m coming** to see you in December.*

going to

- For plans and intentions: *We're **going to** get one tomorrow.*
- For predictions based on what you know or what you can see: *What's the weather **going to** be like? (Look at those clouds. It's **going to** rain.)*

will / shall

- For giving information about the future: *It'**ll** be warm and dry.*
- For predicting what we think or guess will happen: *We'**ll** have a great time!*
- For asking or suggesting what to do (use *shall*): *What **shall** I bring with me?*

Present simple

For timetables and schedules: ***I leave** on the 21st.*

3 Choose the best option.

- a A: What are you doing next Saturday?
  B: I (*go / 'm going*) mountain biking.
  I'm going mountain biking.
- b I've just seen the weather forecast. It (*isn't going to / doesn't*) rain tomorrow.
- c What do you want to do next weekend? (*Shall / Will*) we go fishing?
- d I've looked at the timetable. The train (*leaves / is going to leave*) at 9.30.
- e The beaches are fantastic there. You (*will / shall*) have a great time.

Speaking

4 Work in pairs. Talk about your plans for:

- a this evening
  A: ***What are you doing this evening?***
  B: ***I'm not doing anything special. What about you?***
  A: ***I'm going to watch the football. Do you want to come round and watch it with me? It starts at 7 o'clock.***
  B: ***That would be great. I'll ask my mum if I can come.***
- b next weekend
- c your next holiday

5.7 Improve your writing

In this lesson you will…

- write an advert for outdoor activities in your country.

1 **Work with a partner. Match the outdoor activities to the pictures.**

rock climbing	kite surfing	bungee jumping	snowboarding
surfing	mountain biking	hiking	fishing
kayaking	paragliding	scuba diving	sailing

2 **Make a list of the outdoor activities that you can do in your country.**

3 **Read the advert about outdoor activities in New Zealand on the opposite page. You are going to write an advert for outdoor activities in your country.**

4 **Use the advert about New Zealand as a model for your advert.**

- Have you used a good heading to capture your reader's attention?
- Have you addressed questions directly to your reader?
- Have you used questions, statements and imperatives?
- Have you used the *will* future?
- Have you written captions for your photos?

Write a heading that has impact to capture your reader's attention!

From hiking to sky diving, New Zealand has it all

Address your readers directly with questions to make them want to read more.

Are you interested in seeing new places? Do you dream of going on an activity holiday? Are you keen on trying new things? Then New Zealand is the place for you.

Make suggestions about what visitors might like to do.

Use a variety of verbs and structures: questions, statements, imperatives …

Start in Queenstown, known as the 'Adventure Capital of the World' because it offers every outdoor activity you can think of doing. You might enjoy hiking in the hills and mountains. You may want to spend time fishing or sailing. Perhaps you feel like doing something more energetic, such as kayaking, skiing, snowboarding or mountain biking. Do you fancy trying an extreme sport like bungee jumping or canyoning? If you're really adventurous, perhaps skydiving is for you!

Use the *will* future to make their future trip seem like a reality.

How about swimming with dolphins? Well, think of going to Akaroa Harbour, where you can swim with the world's smallest dolphins. At the end of the day, you can look forward to exploring the Te Anau Glow-worm Caves, where you will see underground waterfalls and more. Imagine visiting a dark area of the caves where thousands of glow-worms light up the space!

Choose a photo or photos to illustrate your advert and write a suitable caption for it.

Are you adventurous? How about trying ziplining in a forest park?

5.8 Project challenge

Project 1: A plan for a day's expedition

You are going to write a plan for a walking trip.

1 Work in groups of four. Read the following details.

- You have to plan a walk that will take at least five hours.
- Choose an area of your country which would be suitable, such as a national park or an area with hiking trails.
- You will be in groups of four, with one adult.
- You each have a backpack measuring 40 cm × 25 cm.

2 Discuss these questions and note down the answers.

a Where are you going to walk?

b What are you going to wear?

c What are you going to put in your backpack? Why might you need those things? Don't make your backpack too heavy! You've got to carry it all day.

d Is there anything else you should think about? (The weather, possible dangers, contact details in case of emergency.)

3 Write your plan under the following headings:

- Where?
- Clothing, equipment
- Other details

4 Exchange your plan with another group's plan. Ask for comments and questions.

- What did you learn from the other group's comments and questions?
- Is there anything in your plan that you would change?

Project 2: An outdoor activity week

Your school is planning an outdoor activity week as part of a 'Great Outdoors' celebration.

Step 1: Find out about an activity centre that you'd like to go to.

Step 2: Prepare a presentation about the centre. Include:

where it is **why it's a good choice** **what you can do there**

Step 3: Give your presentation.

Step 4: Ask the class if they have any questions.

Step 5: Ask the class to give their opinions of your presentation.

- This activity centre is in beautiful countryside, near a large lake.
- It has a fantastic summer programme. There's a Regular Camp Schedule and there's Camp Schedule Plus.
- The Camp Schedule Plus includes a night camping in tents on the hills overlooking the lake.
- There is a variety of activities, so you can choose the ones you are most interested in doing. Here's the programme:

Day 1

Meet and travel

Campsite and team introductions

Dinner round the campfire

Day 2

Some ideas ...

swimming in the lake

night-time canoeing on the lake

raft building

canoeing

canyoning

high ropes

mountain biking

- www – What went well?
- ebi – Even better if …

5.9 Fiction

Hullabaloo in the Guava Orchard by the Indian author, Kiran Desai, tells the story of twenty-year-old Sampath. Sampath has a job at the post office but he finds it boring. He's a dreamer. His father, Mr Chawla, has ambitions for Sampath and wants him to do well in life.

Kiran Desai

38

1 Read and listen to the first extract. Sampath is with his father and his grandmother, Ammaji. He's taking time over his breakfast. How would you describe the tone of this extract – humorous or serious? Give examples to support your answer.

Hullabaloo in the Guava Orchard

"Phoo!" Mr Chawla snorted. "Progress! Ever since he was born, this boy has been progressing steadily in the wrong direction. Instead of trying to work his way upwards, he started on a downward climb and now he is almost as close to the bottom as he could ever be."

"But the world is round," said Ammaji, pleased by her own cleverness. "Wait and see! Even if it appears he is going downhill, he will come up out on the other side. Yes, on top of the world. He is just taking the longer route."

"He is not taking any route, I tell you. He has missed the route altogether. He is just sitting by the side playing with flies." Mr Chawla turned back to Sampath, who had closed his eyes, imagining a long and peaceful sleep in a cool dark place. "Come on," his father urged him. "Get ready for work. It's nine o'clock. Why are you still sitting here like a potato?" He twitched with impatience. "What is the matter with this family? I am the only one with any sense of responsibility, any idea of the way things work in this world."

[0] **hullabaloo:** a lot of excitement and noise surrounding an event

[0] **orchard:** a place where fruit trees are grown

[1] **snorted:** made a loud noise by forcing air out through the nose, like a horse

[2] **steadily:** slowly and gradually

[14] **urged:** strongly advised

[15] **twitched:** made a sudden short, nervous movement

2 **Answer the questions.**

- a Why is Mr Chawla impatient with Sampath this morning?
- b Why do you think Sampath closes his eyes?
- c How would you describe Mr Chawla's attitude to Sampath?
- d How would you describe Ammaji's attitude to Sampath?
- e What impression do we get of Sampath?

Sampath loses his job at the post office. One day he takes a bus out of town and he sees an old orchard in the distance. He jumps off the bus and runs towards a large tree …

39

The tree Sampath had climbed was a guava tree. A guava tree larger and more magnificent than any he had ever seen before. …

How beautiful it was here, how exactly as it should be. This orchard matched something he had imagined all his life: myriad green-skinned globes growing sweet-sour and marvellous upon a hillside with enough trees to fill the eye and enough fruit to scent the air. … Before his eyes, flitting and darting all about him was a flock of parrots, a vivid jewel-green, chattering and shrieking in the highest of spirits. This scene filled his whole mind and he wondered if he could ever get enough of it. This was the way of riches and this was a king's life, he thought … and he ached to swallow it whole, in one glorious mouthful that could become part of him for ever.

[4] myriad: very many
[4] globes: round objects
[7] flock: a group (of birds or sheep)
[7] vivid: very bright
[7] in the highest of spirits: in a very good mood
[10] ached to: wanted to do (something) very much
[10] swallow: make food or drink go down your throat

3 Find the following in the extract:

- a three adjectives that mean 'very good'
- b two verbs to describe the noises parrots make
- c two verbs that describe how parrots move.

Now look up the words in a dictionary to find out exactly what they mean. Remember to look up the infinitive form of the verbs.

4 Values Work in groups. Discuss these questions.

- a Which of the five senses (sight, sound, taste, touch, smell) does the writer use in this second extract? Give examples.
- b Why does the writer use direct speech in the first extract rather than describing what happened?
- c Why does the writer use only descriptive language in the second extract? Whose feelings is she describing – her own or Sampath's?
- d Who understands Sampath better, his father or his grandmother?
- e Do you think the writer is sympathetic towards Sampath?
- f How are Mr Chawla's values different from Sampath's?

When Sampath's father and grandmother find out where Sampath is, they come to take him home, but he refuses to come down from the tree. This is how Kiran Desai starts the scene:

'What are you doing up there?' shouted Mr Chawla. 'Get down at once.'

5 Write the scene that follows. You can use direct speech and descriptive language. You can also reuse words and expressions from the extracts.

Check your progress

General knowledge quiz

How much can you remember about what you have learned?

1 What is this sport called?

2 This sport involves travelling down a fast-flowing river in an inflatable boat. What is called?

3 What are the names of the two main islands in New Zealand?

4 Who are the Māoris?

5 For which country is Aotearoa the Māori name, and what does it mean?

6 Who were Abel Tasman and James Cook and where were they from?

7 What is a kiwi? (Two things.)

8 Who are the All Blacks?

9 Who were the first inhabitants of Australia?

10 What is the capital of Australia?

Vocabulary

Equipment

1 **What are these items?**

a 

b 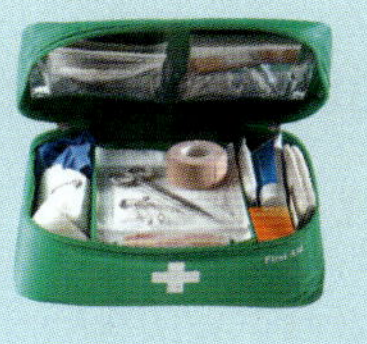

c 

d 

Outdoor pursuits

kayaking surfing hiking
snowboarding swimming waterskiing

2 **Which sport is it?**
Match the sport to the definition.

a You do this in the sea, but without a boat or a sail. If it's cold, you wear a wetsuit. ***surfing***

b You do it on snow, but you don't use skis.

c You do this on water. You are in a boat, but it hasn't got a sail.

d You travel through the water by moving your arms and legs.

e You need a boat to pull you through the water and you should wear a life jacket.

f You walk long distances.

Use of English

1 Correct these sentences.

- **a** I'm interested in learn survival skills.
- **b** We're thinking of go on a camping holiday next year.
- **c** Find your way without a map is difficult.
- **d** I'm no good at put up a tent.
- **e** I think I'll enjoy cook over a campfire.
- **f** Are you good at follow a path or a trail?
- **g** I've always dreamed of see kangaroos in the wild.

2 Choose the correct option.

- **a** The film (***starts*** / *will start*) at 7 o'clock. Don't be late.
- **b** I (*'ll see* / *see*) you tomorrow outside the cinema at 6.45 p.m.
- **c** The weather forecast is really good. It (*isn't going to* / *doesn't*) rain tomorrow.
- **d** Remember, I (*come* / *'m coming*) to see you later.
- **e** I didn't do well in my last spelling test, so I'm (*doing* / *going to do*) really well in the next one.
- **f** What time (*do we have to* / *are we having to*) get the bus for the school trip?

Summary checklist

I can

- ☐ talk about the skills and equipment I might need for outdoor activities.
- ☐ discuss the benefits of spending time in contact with nature.
- ☐ role-play a conversation about what to do in a difficult situation.
- ☐ ask and answer questions about outdoor activities and write a fact file.
- ☐ talk about future plans.
- ☐ write an advert for outdoor pursuits.
- ☐ plan a day's expedition / give a presentation about an activity centre.

6 Sports and games

In this unit you will…

- **talk** about sport, sportspeople and the equipment they use
- **learn** about the qualities needed to succeed in sport (*strength, determination*)
- **talk** about the value of the Paralympic Games, using pronouns such as *everyone, everything, no one*
- **role-play** a quiz about a football match
- **learn** about the ancient Olympics
- **talk** about whether it is fair to use animals in sports
- **write** a profile of a sportsperson.

Getting started

“Which sports and games do you enjoy?”

Watch this!

6.1 The language of sport

In this lesson you will...

- talk about sport, sportspeople and the equipment they use.

- **Why do people do sport?**
  Is international sport important?

Listening

40 **1** **Listen to the commentaries and look at the pictures on these pages. Which sport is it?**

1 horse riding

Vocabulary

2 **Play a vocabulary game with a partner. Take it in turns to define and describe a sportsperson or an item of sports equipment in the pictures on these pages. Your partner has to guess the word.**

A: *You need these when you're riding a horse. You hold them in your hands and they help you to control the horse.*

B: *Reins.*

A: *Yes, that's right. Your turn.*

3 **Play a memory game with a partner. Look at the pictures on these pages for 30 seconds. Then close your book. Can you remember all the words associated with each sport? Make a list.**

Horse riding: rider, reins, saddle

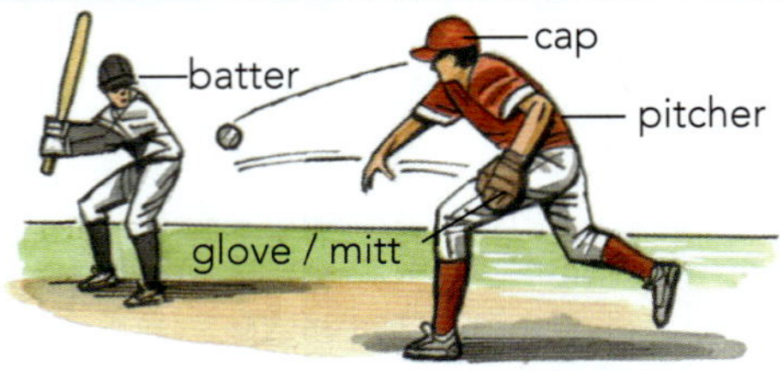

baseball

cricket

golf

cycling

tennis

American football

basketball

horse riding

ice skating

rugby

snowboarding

volleyball

football, soccer

swimming

skateboarding

skiing

Listening

41

4 **Listen to the commentaries and identify the sports.**

1 cricket

Use of English Compound nouns

A compound noun is a noun with another noun, an adjective or a verb before it, for example ***ice hockey***.

5 **Answer the questions.**

a How many compound nouns can you find in the pictures?

b Are there any that have an adjective as the first word?

c How do you express these compound nouns in your language?

Speaking

6 **Work in pairs. Ask and answer the questions in the quiz.**

A question of sport

a What does a football referee do?
A football referee makes sure the players follow the rules.

b What does a goalkeeper do?

c What does a golf caddie do?

d In baseball, who throws the ball and who hits it?

e In cricket, who throws the ball and who hits it?

f In basketball, how do you score points?

g Why is there a net on a tennis court?

h Why are there stumps on a cricket pitch?

6.2 Getting to the top

In this lesson you will...

- learn about the qualities needed to succeed in sport (*strength*, *determination*).

Key words: Physical education

agility
coordination
determination
stamina
strength

- **What do you need to be a top athlete or sportsperson?**

1 **Which sports do you associate with each of the words in the physical education key words box?**

athletics

karate

weightlifting

gymnastics

showjumping

table tennis

hockey

Reading

2 **Read what the sportspeople say. Match them to the pictures in Exercise 1.**

a Balancing on a high beam is difficult. You have to have great confidence in your own ability. You need to be naturally agile but you can improve your agility with practice.

b You need quick reactions and good concentration in this sport, but you also need good hand–eye coordination because you have to coordinate your movements with what you see.

c Speed and determination are essential if you want to win races. You need to be fast and you have to be very determined.

d Being positive and enthusiastic helps you to play well and win matches. Enthusiasm is important for team spirit. Of course, you also need stamina.

e You and your horse both need to have courage, so you must never be afraid of the jumps.

f You have to stay calm and control your emotions. Self-discipline is a key part of martial arts.

g Developing your body to make yourself strong enough is essential, but mental strength is just as necessary. You need to have the confidence that you can do it.

Use of English Abstract nouns

We usually use abstract nouns without *the* or *a / an*.

She had ***strength***, ***agility***, ***coordination*** and ***speed***.

However, when you make an abstract noun specific rather than general, you use *the* or *a / an*.

*You need to have **the confidence** that you can do it.*

3 **Find the abstract nouns in the sentences in Exercise 2 to complete the tables.**

Adjective	Abstract noun
confident	*confidence*
agile	
enthusiastic	
strong	
determined	

Adjective	Abstract noun
fast	
courageous	
self-disciplined	
coordinated	

4 **Complete these sentences with abstract nouns from Exercise 3.**

a Stamina is more important than *speed* for long-distance runners.

b If you can lift a very heavy weight, you have great ....

c If you play a racket sport, you need good hand–eye ....

d If you try very hard to do something difficult, you have great ....

e If you can move your whole body easily and quickly, you have great ....

Speaking

5 **Work in groups. Discuss these questions.**

a What qualities do you need for each of the following sports?

i ice skating **ii** golf **iii** rugby **iv** football **v** tennis

b Which do you think is the most important of these?

c Are some qualities needed for some sports more than others? Give examples.

d Think of sportsmen and sportswomen you admire.
What are the qualities or other factors that have made them successful?

6.3 Sport for all

In this lesson you will...

- talk about the value of the Paralympic Games using pronouns such as *everyone, everything, no one.*

- **What are the Paralympic Games?**

THE WINTER PARALYMPIC GAMES

- Alpine skiing
- Biathlon (cross-country skiing with target shooting)
- Cross-country skiing (also known as Nordic skiing)
- Para-snowboarding
- Ice sledge hockey
- Wheelchair curling

Listening

42 **1 Listen to what some people say about the Winter Paralympics. How do they feel?**

Everything about the Winter Paralympics is brilliant.

Everyone was amazed by the speed, agility and strength of the players.

I've never seen anything like it.

Is there anyone who wasn't inspired by what they saw?

The athletes in the biathlon are an inspiration. Nothing stops them. They make you think no one should ever give up.

The Paralympics are more exciting than the Olympics. Anyone who has seen the snowboarders and the Alpine skiers will tell you that.

Everybody is having a great time. They can't believe what they've seen.

2 Listen again. Then answer the questions.

a Which events do the people talk about?

b Which qualities needed for these events do they talk about?

Use of English Pronouns: *everyone, anyone, no one; everything, anything, nothing*

After these pronouns, we use singular verbs.

Everyone / Everybody *was amazed by the speed, agility and strength of the players.*

Is there ***anyone / anybody*** *who wasn't inspired by what they saw?*

They make you think ***no one / nobody*** *should ever give up.*

Everything *about the Winter Paralympics is brilliant.*

Nothing *stops them.*

'I've never seen ***anything*** *like it.'*

We usually use *anyone* and *anything* with negatives and questions. However, there is a special use of *anyone* and *anything* to mean 'it doesn't matter who / what'.

The Paralympics are more exciting than the Olympics. ***Anyone*** *who has seen the snowboarders and the Alpine skiers will tell you that.*

3 **Complete each sentence about the Paralympics with a word from the box.**

everybody	everything	anyone	anything	nobody	nothing

a There were lots of events going on at the same time, but ***everything*** was very well organised.

b The opening ceremony was brilliant. I've never seen .... like it.

c It was a fantastic event. .... was really happy to be there.

d We all got tickets, so .... was disappointed.

e A lot of people bought souvenirs like T-shirts and baseball caps. At the end of the evening, there was .... left.

f I was amazed that .... could go so fast in a wheelchair.

Speaking

4 **Work in small groups. Talk about an event you've enjoyed. It can be a sports event or any other kind of event.**

a What was the event?

b When and where did it take place?

c What was the atmosphere like?

d Give your impressions.

It was brilliant / exciting / amazing

Everybody / Nobody was …

Everything / Nothing …

5 **Discuss the following questions.**

a Has the attitude to disability generally changed in recent years?

b What role have events like the Paralympic Games had in changing attitudes and opinions?

6.4 The final score

In this lesson you will...

- learn the vocabulary needed to describe a game of football
- role-play a quiz about a football match.

- **Why is football the most popular sport in the world?**

Vocabulary

1 **Read the football glossary. The meanings of six of the words or phrases are given below. Which six?**

a match	a goal	extra time
(team A) against (team B)	3:0 up (three–nil up)	full-time
to score	the first half	a penalty shoot-out
the score	the second half	to win on penalties
half-time	a draw (e.g. 3:3 = three–all)	to win (*past tense, won*)

a a game between two teams ***a match***
b to get a goal or points in a game
c the interval between two parts of a match
d the time after the interval in a match
e when both teams have the same number of goals at the end of a match
f an additional number of minutes that you play after 90 minutes to find the winner

Listening

43 2 **Listen to this extract from a TV sports quiz programme. Which of the pictures on the next page does it refer to?**

3 **Listen again and look at the picture you chose in answer to Exercise 2. Answer the questions.**

a Who was playing in the match?

b What happened in the first minute of the game?

c And then what happened before half-time?

d Who scored the goals?

e What was the score at half-time?

f What happened in the second half? Who scored?

g What was the score at the end of the second half?

h Who won in the end? How?

Speaking

4 **In small groups, role-play the TV quiz. One of you is the quizmaster and the others answer the questions.**

44

5 **Work in pairs. Look at the scoreboard of the other match. Have a conversation about the match.**
You can listen to a model conversation to help you. Start like this:

Who was playing in the match?

6.5 The ancient Olympics

In this lesson you will...

- learn about the ancient Olympics
- find information about the modern Olympic Games and compare them with the ancient Olympics.

Key words: Physical education

biathlon
decathlon
pentathlon
triathlon

- **Do you think the Olympic Games are a good idea? Give your reasons.**

Reading

1 **Read about the ancient Olympics on the opposite page. Find three things you didn't already know.**

2 **Answer the questions.**

a Where and when did the first Olympics take place?

b What was a *stadion*?

c What was there at the beginning and end of the five-day Olympics?

d How many sports were there in the pentathlon and what were they?

e How did competitors prepare for the Games?

f Did women take part in sport in Ancient Greece? How do you know?

g Were the ancient Olympics popular? How do you know?

3 **Answer the questions about the words in the physical education key words box.**

a In the Winter Paralympics, there is a *biathlon*. Athletes do cross-country skiing and shooting, so what do you think *biathlon* means?

b How many events are there in a *triathlon, a pentathlon, a decathlon*?

Speaking

4 **Work with a partner. How much do you know about the modern Olympic Games? Answer these questions. Use the internet or a reference book to help you.**

a How often do they take place?

b Where are they held?

c How long do they last?

d How many sports and events are there?

e What happens at the beginning and end of the games?

5 **Discuss this question: What are the similarities and differences between the ancient Olympics and the modern Olympics?**

The ancient Olympics

The ancient Olympics began in 776 BCE in Olympia in Greece and they took place there every four years until 394 CE. The first Games were a one-day event and had just one running race, the *stadion*, a short sprint of between 180 and 240 metres – the length of the stadium. The first-ever Olympic race was won by a cook called Koroibos.

The Games were popular, and in about 400 BCE they were extended to five days, with an opening and a closing ceremony. At the end of the second day, the pentathlon took place: discus, javelin and long jump followed by running and finally wrestling. There were also boxing matches, chariot races and horse races.

The athletes trained for at least ten months in a gymnasium before they arrived to compete in the Games. Winning was everything. There were no medals, no prizes and no second or third places. However, back in his home city, the winner received money and vats of olive oil; he got the best seats at the theatre; and he probably never worked again.

Women didn't take part in the ancient Olympics but they had their own women-only Games, which took place every four years.

Forty thousand spectators arrived in Olympia to watch the Games. They came by land and by sea and they came from places as far away as Spain, Italy and Egypt.

On the final day of the Games, the champions were crowned with olive wreaths and there was a feast for all of the competitors.

6.6 Racing to win

In this lesson you will...

- listen to opinions about animals in sport
- talk about whether it is fair to use animals in sports.

- **Which animals are used in sports?**

Listening

45

1 **Listen to the radio programme. What is the discussion about?**

2 **Listen again. Then answer the questions.**

a What speed can a racehorse reach?

b What speed can a camel reach in a short race?

c Which can run faster over short distances, a horse or a camel?

d Which is better for a long journey, a horse or a camel? Why?

e What are Adel's two main reasons for being against horse and camel racing?

f Which examples does Lauren give to say why horseracing is not necessarily wrong?

Use of English Comparative adverbs

The following comparatives are irregular:

adverb	comparative
well	better
badly	worse
far	further

Short adverbs usually have comparative forms ending in *-er*.

fast	**faster**	**high**	**higher**
hard	**harder**	**long**	**longer**

Use *much* and *far* to give emphasis in a comparison:

In the past, horses got injured and exhausted ***much more frequently****.*

Horses get injured and exhausted ***far less frequently*** *now than in the past.*

You can compare two things that are not equal like this:

Camels don't run ***as fast as*** *horses.*

Camels are ridden by small robots. The camels can hear instructions from their owners during the race.

3 Complete the sentences using comparative adverbs from the Use of English box.

a We rode for two kilometres yesterday but we rode for ten kilometres today. We rode much *further* today than we did yesterday.

b In the high jump I can jump a metre, but my friend can jump a metre and a half. My friend can jump .... than I can.

c You swim well, but your sister's a really good swimmer. Your sister swims .... than you.

d I can run 100 metres in 20 seconds, but my cousin can run it in 15 seconds. I can't run the 100 metres .... my cousin can.

e It takes me ten minutes to get to the running track but it takes my friend an hour. It takes my friend much .... to get to the running track than it takes me.

Speaking

4 Work in groups. Discuss this question:
Is it fair to use animals in sports? Use the language in the box to help you.

Language of discussion

Asking for opinions

What do you think about …?

Why do you think …?

Giving opinions

I think / I don't think …

It seems to me that …

Asking for and giving clarification

What do you mean when you say …?

I'm not sure what you mean.

Can you explain what you mean?

I mean …

Giving examples

For example, …

Introducing a contrasting idea

However, …

Interrupting

Could I just say that …?

Hold on a minute, …

Agreeing / disagreeing

I agree / I don't agree …

That's true but …

I see what you mean, but …

Summarising

So you're saying that …

In other words, …

Giving further opinions

I'd also say that …

6.7 Improve your writing

In this lesson you will...

- write a profile of a sportsperson.

1 **Read the profile of a sportsperson on the opposite page. Where might you find it? In a novel? In a sports magazine? In a sports reference book?**

2 **Match each of the following to a number in the text on the opposite page.**

a name *2*
b nationality
c date of birth
d sport
e disability
f Paralympic debut
g quote from the athlete
h inspiration
i attractions of the sport

3 **Write an account of a sportsperson. Use the following information and the text on the opposite page as a model.**

Nationality: British

Name: Kare Adenegan

Sport: wheelchair para-athletics

Paralympic debut: 2016 Rio de Janeiro

Disability: has cerebral palsy

Date of birth: 29 December 2000

Inspiration: wasn't allowed to do any sport at school; watching Paralympic Games 2012 inspired her

Kare Adenegan (right) with Hannah Cockcroft

Attractions of the sport: speed and power

Quotes: 'I want to continue to train hard and dedicate my time and energy to my sport.'

'Whatever happens, I'll be happy as long as I've done my best.'

- In the first paragraph, have you included the athlete's name, nationality, sport, the date of his / her debut in the sport and his / her disability?
- In the second paragraph, have you included the athlete's date of birth, his / her inspiration and what attracted him / her to the sport?
- In the third paragraph, have you used a quote from the athlete?

1, 2 The Chinese para-athlete, Sun Qi,
is one of the biggest names on the
3 para-snowboarding scene. He made his
Paralympic debut at the Paralympics in
4 South Korea in 2018. This is particularly
5 impressive for someone who lost his lower
right leg as a result of a firework explosion.

6 Sun Qi, who was born in 1999, didn't start
out as a snowboarder. He competed in
7 para-cycling first. His coach inspired him to
take up para-snowboarding. He fell in love
8 with the speed and intensity of the sport.

9 'I focus on myself and on improving my skills,' he says. 'Yes, I watch other snowboarders competing, to learn from them and get better. They are all very talented and sharing races with them will make me a better athlete.'

6.8 Project challenge

Project 1: A classroom display

You are going to research a sport and make a classroom display about it.

1 Which sport does this picture show? What do you know about the sport?

2 Work in small groups. You're going to produce a classroom display about one of your country's national sports. First, choose your sport.

Which sport shall we choose?

Do we all think that's a good idea?

Let's find out if another group's doing the same sport.

3 Do your research. Answer these questions.

a Where is this sport played?
b How many players are there?
c What equipment do they need?
d What do they wear?
e How long is a game?
f Is it divided into two halves?
g How are points scored?
h Which are the best-known teams?
i Who are the best-known players?
j What skills do you need to be a good player?

4 Decide how to plan, organise and produce the work. Then create your display.

a Who is going to design the display?
b Who is going to find the pictures?
c Who is going to do the illustrations?
d Who is going to write the text?

- Make constructive comments about other groups' displays.
- Can you think of anything that would make the display even better than it is?

Project 2: A presentation

You are going to give a presentation about the history of a sport.

1. Work in groups. You're going to give a presentation about the history of a sport that's popular in your country. Decide on the sport.
2. Read and discuss the first part of this presentation about skiing.

   Is this a good way to start?

a

The origins of skiing

Skiing has a long history. Before skiing was a sport, skis were used by Scandinavian farmers, hunters and warriors to get around on snow.

b

The picture shows two warriors on skis carrying the two-year-old future king of Norway in 1206, to a place of safety.

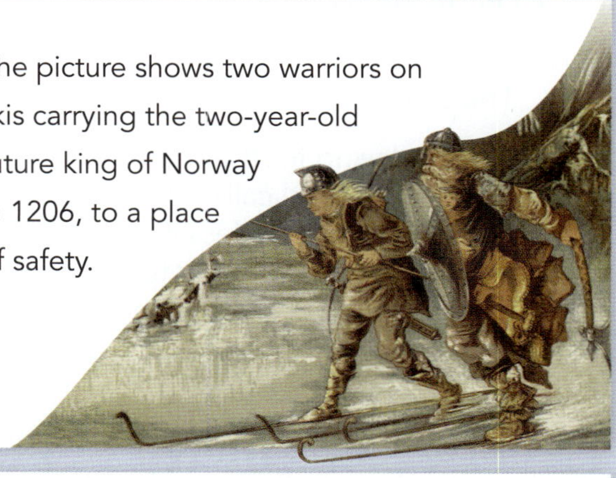

c

How skiing became a sport

In the late 18th century, skis were used by soldiers in Norway, Sweden and Denmark for military exercises. They also organised competitions in which they had to ski downhill and shoot at targets.

d

The first public skiing competition was in Tromsø in Norway in 1843.

3. Prepare your presentation. It can be a digital presentation or it can be on paper.

- www – What went well?
- ebi – Even better if …

6.9 Fiction

Bend it like Beckham, by Narinder Dhami, is the story of Jess, a girl who loves football. Her hero is the famous footballer, David Beckham. As she says, 'No one can bend a ball like Beckham.'

46

1 Read the summary of the story so far, and read and listen to the extract from Chapter 2 on the opposite page. Who is the narrator ('I') in the story?

> **The story so far**
>
> Jess is playing football in the park with her friend Taz and his friends. A girl called Jules introduces herself. She's noticed how good Jess is at football and invites her to a training session with her team, the Hounslow Harriers. At the training session, Jess meets Joe, the team's coach.

2 Find these football words in the text.

- a moved the ball forward with short kicks
- b the players who try to stop you reaching the goal
- c the area in front of the goal
- d kicked with the side of the foot
- e it's attached to the goalposts to stop the ball

3 Find these expressions in the text. What do they mean?

- a (I was) grinning from ear to ear. (line 6)
- b I beamed. (line 12)
- c He frowned. (line 13)
- d My face fell. (line 20)
- e I glowed with pride. (lines 53–54)

4 Read the text again and answer these questions.

- a How does Jess feel before she goes on to the pitch?
- b How does she feel when she's on the pitch?
- c How does she feel when she comes off the pitch?
- d How does Joe's attitude to Jess change and why?

> 3 rushed: hurried
>
> 10 (it would have sounded) really off: very unfriendly
>
> 15 I felt a bit of a fool: I felt silly
>
> 22 (I thought he was going to) chuck me out: make me leave
>
> 26 to give me a go: give me a chance
>
> 32 the Harriers strip: the shirt and shorts worn by the Harriers team
>
> 38 that lot: those people
>
> 48 yelling: shouting loudly
>
> 57 if I'd made it into the side: if I'd been successful in getting into the team
>
> 59 I'd set up goals: I'd made it possible for someone to score goals
>
> 60 trooped off: walked off together in a group
>
> 61 lurch: suddenly move in a way that is not controlled
>
> 64 gasped: breathed quickly and deeply

Bend it Like Beckham

I took a deep breath, and ran out on to the pitch. Jules had stopped to chat to Joe as I rushed over to them. The first thing I noticed was that Joe didn't look too pleased to see me. But that couldn't stop me grinning from ear to ear. I was excited just to be there.

"Where do you usually play?" Joe said. No hello, nothing. It would have sounded really off, if he hadn't had such a soft Irish accent.

I beamed at him. "In the park."

He looked at Jules and frowned. "I meant, what position?"

"Oh, sorry." I felt a bit of a fool. "I usually play all over, but up front on the right is best."

Joe looked me up and down. "Get your boots on, then," he said.

My face fell. "I haven't got any."

For a minute, I thought he was going to chuck me out before I'd even got started. I stared at him anxiously, trying to make him realise how desperate I was to play. Jules was looking a bit uncomfortable. I guessed that she'd had to persuade Joe to give me a go.

"All right," he said at last. "Join in and start warming up." I smiled with relief, and unzipped my tracksuit top. I had my Beckham shirt on underneath. Maybe soon I'd be wearing the Harriers strip like the other girls. But first I had to show what I could do ...

I felt nervous as I took my place on the pitch with the other players. I never felt nervous when I was playing against Taz and that lot, but this was different. I had to do well to earn a place in the side.

But once the ball was at my feet, I lost all my nerves. It was just like being back in the park. Adrenaline pumped through me as I dribbled down the pitch, managing to avoid two defenders. I did my famous double-step over the ball to get round a third and ran forward. I had the goal in my sights.

"Pass to Jules!" I heard Joe yelling from the touchline.

I slid the ball across the box, straight into Jules' path, and she sidefooted it into the net.

"Brilliant!" Joe called, and I glowed with pride. I wanted this so much it *hurt*.

When the game was over, I was so nervous, I felt sick. I wanted to know if I'd made it into the side. I *thought* I'd done well – I hadn't scored myself but I'd set up goals for Jules and another girl whose name I didn't know. As we trooped off the pitch, I felt my heart lurch as Joe came over to me and took me to one side.

"How'd it feel out there?" he asked.

"Excellent," I gasped. I was red in the face and out of breath but I felt fantastic. "Really great."

Joe looked at me curiously. "I've never seen an Indian girl into football."

I smiled shyly at him. "I would have come sooner, but I didn't even know they had a girls' team here."

The day our first match of the summer tournament against Chiswick came round, I felt nervous, but I couldn't wait to get out on to the pitch. This wasn't like playing in the park, or the games in our training sessions. This was the real thing.

"All right, Jess?" Joe asked me quietly as we filed out of the changing rooms.

I blushed, and Jules, who was just ahead of me, turned round curiously to look at us. Don't ask me why I went red, I don't know – I just did. "Yeah, no problem," I muttered.

"OK, go out there and do your stuff," Joe said, and turned away.

And, suddenly, when I was out on the pitch, everything seemed to come together. Joining the Harriers had been the best thing in my whole life so far, and I'd loved the training sessions, pushing myself harder and getting better and better. But out on the pitch, playing a real game, was what it was all about. Adrenaline raced through me as the ball was placed in the centre circle, ready for the kick-off. I was up for this and I was going to do my best.

Mel was right. Chiswick had a great defence, and it took us a while to break them down. About halfway through the second half, Jules slotted the ball through to me, opening up a gap between two defenders. I ran through and banged the ball into the net. One-nil.

"Yes!" I yelled. My first goal in a proper, real-life match! I was so excited, I cartwheeled across the pitch and finished off with a backflip. As the other girls rushed to congratulate me, I looked over at Joe. He was grinning at me and I glowed with pride.

By the time we'd won the match two-nil, with another goal from Mel, I knew that there was no going back. I couldn't give this up.

5 Read and listen to the second extract and answer the questions.

- **a** This is the first match of the summer tournament. How do we know that it's Jess's first match? How does her mood change and why?
- **b** Which words and phrases give a sense of excitement?

6 Imagine the scene after the match. Jess is talking to the other girls and to Joe, their coach. Write the scene.

Start like this: ***After the match, we all …***

- Start a new paragraph when each person talks.
- Use inverted commas at the beginning (") and at the end (") of what someone says.

Writing tip

Follow the style of the extract.

Notice how the writer uses short paragraphs and mixes narrative and direct speech.

Check your progress

General knowledge quiz

How much can you remember about what you have learned?

1 Bowler, batsman, ball, stumps … What's the sport?

2 What are the Winter Paralympics?

3 What do you call the interval between the two halves of a football match?

4 What do you call the result of a football match in which both teams have scored the same number of goals?

5 Where and how often did the ancient Olympics take place?

6 What type of race was a *stadion*?

7 What did the winner at the ancient Olympics receive? (two things)

8 Wrestling was one of the events in the pentathlon. What were the other four?

9 Who were not allowed to take part in the ancient Olympic Games?

10 What is this and where would you find it?

Vocabulary

Sports and sports equipment

1 **Choose the odd one out and give your reason in each case.**

a i footballer ii referee iii goalkeeper iv bowler

Referee (ii) is the odd one out because the others are all sports players.

OR

Bowler (iv) is the odd one out because a bowler is connected with cricket, whereas all the others are connected with football.

b i boxing ii cricket iii rugby iv football

c i golfer ii batsman iii rider iv snowboard

d i elbow pads ii knee pads iii helmet iv reins

2 **Complete the match report.**

Galatasaray became champions of the Turkish Super League after winning their match ***against*** Istanbul Basaksehir on Sunday in Istanbul. The final ……… was 2-1.

Basaksehir's Riad Bajic ……… the opening goal in the 17th minute of the ……… at Galatasaray's Turk Telekom Stadium.

The first ……… ended 1-0.

Galatasaray were the stronger team in the ……… half, with goals from Sofiane Feghouli in the 47th minute and Henry Onyekuru in the 64th minute.

Use of English

1 Complete the second sentence by changing the adjective from the first sentence to an abstract noun.

a She's a very successful athlete.
She enjoyed *success* at an early age.

b You need to be strong to be good at most sports.
.... is important for most sports.

c Gymnasts have to be very agile.
One of the most important qualities for a gymnast is ....

d Are you determined to succeed?
Do you have enough .... to be successful?

2 Complete the sentences using a pronoun beginning with *every-*, *any-* or *no-*.

a *Everyone* knows the answer to that question. It's really easy.

b I've got tickets for Saturday's match. Is .... interested?

c I'm bored. There's .... to do.

d I didn't buy .... because I didn't have any money.

e It was a really difficult maths problem. .... got the answer right.

3 Complete the sentences with a comparative adverb using the prompts in brackets.

a The winner of the javelin competition is the athlete who throws the javelin *further* (*far*) than the other athletes.

b The 100 metres winner is the sprinter who runs .... (*fast*) than the other athletes.

c The high jump is won by the athlete who jumps .... (*high*) than anyone else.

d Mo Farah was disappointed with his time in this year's Berlin Marathon because he didn't run as .... (*fast*) he ran last year.

e I felt quite sure of myself yesterday when I was skiing, but today I skied far .... (*confident*), which is why I fell several times.

Summary checklist

I can

- ☐ talk about a range of sports, sportspeople and sports equipment.
- ☐ discuss the qualities needed to succeed in different sports.
- ☐ talk about the value of Paralympic sports.
- ☐ describe a game of football.
- ☐ compare the ancient Olympics with the modern Olympics.
- ☐ discuss whether it is fair to use animals in sports.
- ☐ write a profile of a sportsperson.
- ☐ make a classroom display / give a presentation about a sport.

7 Success

In this unit you will...

- **describe** what people do in their jobs
- **read** and **talk** about how science can improve people's lives
- **listen** to people with disabilities talking about problems in everyday life
- **use** adjectives to describe personality
- **read** about and discuss the success of a young rider
- **listen** to people answering a personality quiz
- **write** a profile of yourself.

Getting started

"Think of three people who have been successful. What can you say about them?"

Watch this!

7.1 At work

In this lesson you will...

- learn and use vocabulary for jobs
- describe what people do in their jobs.

- **What jobs do people in your family do?**

Vocabulary

1 **Match the people to what they do.**

lawyer
accountant
architect
pharmacist
plumber
vet
dentist
designer
soldier
pilot

a can show how things like clothes, furniture and gardens will look
b designs buildings
c flies a plane
d advises people about the law and acts for them in a law court
e gives medical care to sick animals
f is part of the army of a country
g keeps records of money which people or companies earn and spend
h looks after your teeth
i prepares medicine in a pharmacy or hospital
j repairs and connects water pipes

2 **Check your answers with a partner.**

A: A lawyer advises people about the law and acts for them in a law court.

B: Yes, that's right.

3 **Write similar definitions for the following jobs. Then compare your answers with your partner's answers.**

a nurse
b car mechanic
c hairdresser
d police officer
e chef
f electrician
g firefighter
h receptionist
i teacher
j waiter / waitress

Listening

48

4 **Listen. What kind of radio programme is it?**

5 **Listen again. What jobs do the people do? Write down the answers.**

6 **Work with a partner. Write a short dialogue for another job. Role-play it to the class. The other students have to guess what the job is.**

7 **Work with a partner. Look at the picture. Choose five people and say what you think they do. Your partner has to guess which person you're describing.**

A: *I think this person works for a social media company.*

B: *Is it this person, with the long dark hair and the blue jumper?*

A: *Yes, it is.*

Language tip

If you're not sure how to say what job a person does, you can say:

He / She works **in** *finance / marketing / IT (information technology).*

He / She works **in** *an office / a bank / a shop.*

He / She works **for** *a social media company / a fashion company.*

Speaking

8 **Work with a partner. Ask and answer.**

A: *Which of the jobs on these pages would you like to do?*

B: *I think I'd like to be …*

I'd like to work in …

I'd like to work for …

A: *Why?*

7.2 Making science work

In this lesson you will...

- read and talk about how science can improve people's lives
- use adjectives followed by prepositions (*good at, proud of*).

Key words: Science and technology

device
hydroelectric generator
inventor
propeller
prototype
scientist
turbine

- **If you're good at science and technology, what jobs might you do in the future?**

Reading

1 **Read the text. What did Hannah do and why?**

Hannah Herbst is a young scientist and inventor who wants to make a difference to people's lives.

When Hannah was 9, she started writing to a penfriend in Ethiopia. She was surprised to learn that her penfriend, Ruth, had no electricity in her home, so it was hard for her to read and do her homework. Later, when Hannah was at Wharton High School, she became very interested in science and decided to try to help Ruth.

Hannah came up with the idea of a device with a propeller and a hydroelectric generator. Her invention converts the movement of the ocean into energy in order to produce electricity. She built a prototype that showed how this could work, and it won the Discovery Education 3M Young Scientist Challenge. 'This prototype is very novel because it's portable,' she said. 'Most of the turbines available on the market are large and they cost thousands to millions of dollars, whereas mine costs less than $500 to make.'

Hannah wants to encourage other students to get involved in science. 'My biggest challenge,' Hannah said, 'was getting started. I was really involved in theatre and athletics, and I'm still really passionate about those things.' She was worried she wouldn't have time for everything. Her advice is 'start small and work your way up from there'.

Vocabulary

2 Look at the words in the science and technology key words box. Answer the questions.

- **a** Which two words describe people?
- **b** Which three words describe pieces of equipment?
- **c** Which word means 'the first version of something', 'a sort of model'?
- **d** Which word means a 'piece of mechanical or electronic equipment'?

3 Complete the second sentence so that it means the same as the first sentence.

- **a** My biggest challenge was getting started.
  The most .... thing was starting (in engineering).
  interesting / difficult / exciting
- **b** I was really involved in theatre and athletics.
  I did .... theatre and athletics. *a little / some / a lot of*
- **c** I'm still really passionate about those things.
  .... those things. *I'm not interested in / I continue to be very enthusiastic about / I don't enjoy*
- **d** Just give something a go.
  Just .... doing something.
  try / stop / talk about

4 Use the adjectives in the Use of English box to write six sentences that are true for you.

I'm quite good at ... ***I'm worried about ...*** ***I'm proud of ...***

Use of English adjective + preposition

Some adjectives are followed by prepositions. Here are some useful ones.

good / bad **at**

excited / happy / worried / nervous **about**

proud / frightened / aware / tired / full **of**

similar / kind **to**

responsible **for**

interested / involved **in**

keen **on**

Speaking

5 Work in groups. Discuss these questions.

- **a** How can Hannah's invention help Ruth?
- **b** How is Hannah's invention different from similar devices that already exist?
- **c** What advice does Hannah give for people interested in science? Do you think it's good advice?
- **d** How can scientists make a difference to people's lives?

7.3 A young entrepreneur

In this lesson you will...

- listen to people with disabilities talking about problems in everyday life
- use adjectives followed by the infinitive (*happy to try something new*).

- **An entrepreneur is a person who has an idea for something new and starts their own business. Can you think of anyone who has done this?**

Reading

1 **Read about Alex Knoll. What was Alex's idea? How did he know it was a good idea?**

Alex is still at school but he already has his own company. He has come up with the idea for an app that helps people with disabilities. Alex had the idea when he saw a man in a wheelchair trying to open a heavy door. His idea was very simple. What the man needed was an app that told him which shops, cafés and other places had automatic doors. Alex appeared on a TV programme to talk about his idea. After the programme, he had 30,000 emails from viewers, telling him how pleased they were to hear about his app and how it would change their lives.

'I'm going to work as hard as I can, as fast as I can, to get it done and get it out to the people,' he said.

Listening

49

2 **Listen to four people talking. What do they have in common?**

3 **Listen again. For each person, answer these questions.**

a What is their disability?

b How can Alex's app help them?

c Which people have tried the app already?

d Which people haven't tried it yet?

Use of English adjective + infinitive

Some adjectives can be followed by the infinitive (with *to*), especially adjectives that express feelings, opinions and reactions to situations.

I was really ***pleased to hear*** *about this app.*

Alex was really ***clever to come up with*** *the idea.*

It's ***embarrassing to ask*** *people to read the menu for you.*

It's very ***disappointing to go*** *to the theatre and not to be able to hear what the actors are saying.*

It's ***impossible to get into*** *some places.*

It's ***hard to read*** *the menu.*

It's really ***useful to know*** *which places welcome people with guide dogs.*

4 Use the phrases in the two columns to write ten sentences. They can be serious or amusing!

a	It's wrong	to get 95% in the English exam.
b	It's difficult	to get up early to go swimming.
c	It's good	to go.
d	It was crazy	to hear that the match was cancelled because of the rain.
e	It's interesting	to meet people from other countries.
f	I was surprised	to spend all that money on a pair of shoes.
g	I'm sometimes afraid	to stand on one leg with your eyes closed.
h	I'm happy	to talk in front of a lot of other people.
i	I'm ready	to talk to a friend when you've got a problem.
j	I'm sorry	to tell lies.

5 Compare your sentences with the sentences other students have written.

6 Work in two teams. Take turns to choose a phrase from a to e in Exercise 4. The other team has five seconds to complete it in any way they choose. It can be serious or amusing.

7.4 What are you like?

In this lesson you will…

- use adjectives to describe personality
- use verbs followed by *-ing*.

- **What are you like? Choose three adjectives that describe you.**

  friendly, sporty, quiet, …

50 **1 Listen to the conversation. Choose the two adjectives that describe each person.**

a Charlotte's older brother — **patient easy-going serious logical**

b Sophie — **shy independent modest adventurous**

c Sophie's older sister — **organised sociable hard-working friendly**

d Charlotte — **determined optimistic decisive calm**

51 **2 Listen and repeat. Make sure you put the stress on the correct syllable.**

First syllable stress	Second syllable stress	Third syllable stress
patient	adventurous	independent
serious	decisive	optimistic
sociable	determined	easy-going
modest	hard-working	
logical		
friendly		
organised		

Listening tip

Prepare to listen by looking for clues about what you're going to hear. In Exercise 1, you know it's a conversation in which people are talking about members of their family. You know you're going to hear two words that describe the personality of each of them. Who are the four people?

If you don't know what some of the words in the question mean, ask your teacher. For example, *'What does "easy-going" mean?'*

Listening

52 **3 These people have all been asked the same question. What do you think it is?**

4 Listen again. Choose a job for each person. Think about their personalities and interests. (Look at the lists in Lesson 7.1 to help you. There can be more than one answer.)

Use of English verb + *-ing*

After some verbs, we use the *-ing* form.

I'd like a job that ***involves working*** *with young people.*

I ***don't mind explaining*** *things to people.*

appreciate	consider	fancy	hate	practise
avoid	detest	feel like	imagine	risk
can't face	dislike	finish	involve	spend time
can't help	don't mind	give up	keep on	suggest
can't stand	enjoy			

5 Listen again and complete the sentences with words in the *-ing* form.

a She'd like a job that involves *working* with young people.

She doesn't mind .... things to people.

She doesn't fancy .... in an office.

b His parents suggested .... to university to study medicine.

He can't imagine .... in a hospital.

c She's considered .... the emergency services.

She enjoys .... people.

She knows you risk .... in difficult and dangerous situations.

She doesn't mind .... a challenge.

d He can't stand .... early.

He doesn't fancy .... in an office.

He spends a lot of time .... and painting.

e She knows you have to spend time .... and taking exams.

She thinks she can keep on .... to get all her qualifications.

Writing

6 The people in Exercise 3 were asked: 'What kind of job do you want to do in the future?' How would you answer that question? Write your reply using adjectives from Exercise 1 and the verbs followed by *-ing* from the Use of English box.

7.5 Making history

In this lesson you will...

- read about and discuss the success of a young rider
- use verbs followed by the infinitive.

[22] **to be blocked in:** to be unable to move because something is stopping you

[25] **to pull out:** to move to the side, as a car would in order to pass a car in front of it

[29] **to be over the moon:** an idiom meaning to be very happy

[31] **to make the news:** an idiom meaning to appear in newspapers or in the media

- **What personal qualities do you need to be a good rider?**

Reading

1 Read the article. How would you describe Khadijah's personality?

An 18-year-old girl wins at Goodwood … and makes history

Khadijah Mellah, a teenager from south London, has won the Magnolia Cup. She was the first woman wearing a hijab to compete at a British race meeting. What makes the success even more amazing was that she only started riding a racehorse very recently. 'I only sat on a racehorse a couple of months ago and I am just never going to forget this day. To be honest, I want to go back and do it all over again. What an incredible feeling!'

Growing up in a big city, Khadija didn't have many opportunities to be with horses. However, her parents found a riding school called The Ebony Horse Club. They encouraged her to take lessons there. A television presenter met Khadijah at the riding club and invited her to take part in the Magnolia Cup.

She spent two months training at the British Racing School in Newmarket before competing in the race. Her trainer only allowed her to take part when he knew she was good enough. He advised Khadijah to stay in the middle of the group during the race. However, she soon found she was blocked in by the horses in front. 'There were three horses in front of me, like a brick wall … I didn't know what to do, so I thought, I'll pull out and see what happens.'

The next thing she knew, she'd crossed the finishing line in first place. 'I'm quite competitive, so I wanted to win this race but I never expected to. My parents have been really happy, completely over the moon for me.'

Khadijah has made the news in France, Turkey, Australia, Saudi Arabia, Indonesia and South Africa. 'I've spent a lot of time talking to people about my race. It's been a busy few days.' In a TV interview she said: 'I can't wait to hear a success story where someone says, actually Khadijah Mellah's been a role model to me.'

Khadijah thinks it's important for girls to be ambitious. 'From a young age I have wanted to be the person that people look up to,' she said. 'I have already started receiving other messages from Muslim girls. It makes me really happy to hear from all these people that I've affected positively.'

2 **Copy and complete this summary of the article.**

Name: **Khadijah Mellah**	
Age:	Recent success (What? Where?):
Home city:	Family's reactions:
Riding experience:	Media attention:

Key words: Citizenship

to be a role model
to inspire someone

3 **Answer the questions.**

- **a** Why is Khadijah's success in the news?
- **b** What do you learn about her family?
- **c** How do you think her personality has contributed to her success?
- **d** Is she a good role model? Why?
- **e** How could Khadijah's achievement influence others?

Use of English verb + infinitive, verb + object + infinitive

After some verbs, we use the infinitive with *to*. For example: *agree, decide, plan, aim, hope, learn, want.*

I ***want to go back*** *and do it all over again.*

After some verbs you can put an object between the verb and the infinitive. For example:

advise, allow, ask, encourage, expect, help, invite, inspire, like, prefer, promise, want.

They ***encouraged*** *her* ***to take*** *lessons.*

4 **Complete these sentences. You can look back at the article to help you.**

- **a** A television presenter ………… Khadijah to take part in the Magnolia Cup.
- **b** Khadijah's trainer only ………… her to take part when he knew she was good enough.
- **c** The trainer ………… Khadijah to stay in the middle of the group during the race.
- **d** Khadijah never ………… to win.
- **e** She can't ………… to hear a success story where someone says, actually Khadijah Mellah's been a role model to me.

5 **Write sentences that are true for you.**

Use a suitable infinitive.

- **a** I've always wanted …
- **b** When I'm older I plan …
- **c** I hope …
- **d** I'd like to learn …

Use an object + infinitive.

- **e** My family have always encouraged …
- **f** My parents allow …
- **g** On special occasions, we invite …
- **h** I sometimes help …

6 **Work in groups. Discuss the questions.**

- **a** Who do you think of as a good role model?
- **b** Who inspires you? Is that person a role model for you?

7.6 Personality quiz

In this lesson you will...

- listen to people answering a personality quiz
- ask and answer questions in a personality quiz.

- **Why do you think personality quizzes are popular?**

Listening

53 **1** **Listen to Maya and Amir doing the first section of the quiz. What impression do you get of Amir? What sort of person is he?**

54 **2** **Listen to Maya and Amir doing the second section of the quiz. What impression do you get of Maya? What sort of person is she?**

Speaking

3 **Work in pairs. Ask and answer the questions in the first and second sections of the quiz. Make notes of your partner's answers.**

55 **4** **Ask and answer the rest of the questions in the quiz. (You can listen to Maya and Amir doing the rest of the quiz to help you.) Make notes of your partner's answers.**

5 **Try the quiz again. Can you improve or add more detail to your answers?**

6 **Look at the notes you made. Tell the other students in the class about your partner. Can you use any of the adjectives from Lesson 7.4?**

7 **What do you think about personality quizzes? Are they useful?**

Speaking tip

Useful phrases for answering questions

I don't really know.

It depends.

I suppose …

Let me think.

Yes, definitely. / No, definitely not!

No, not really.

It's all about you!

Try this quiz to find out more about yourself and what you might do in the future.

FREE TIME

1 Do you enjoy playing team sports or do you prefer individual activities like swimming or running?

2 How much time do you spend playing games on your computer every day?

3 Are you keen on making things? What sort of things?

4 Do you find it easy to fill your free time? Do you ever get bored?

AIMS AND AMBITIONS

5 Would you like to live in another country?

6 Would you consider studying abroad?

7 What subjects do you hope to study when you're older?

8 Are money and status important to you?

PERSONAL STRENGTHS

9 Do you get nervous about trying something new?

10 When you promise to do something, do you always do it?

11 Do people ever ask you to help them when they have a problem?

12 Do you mind making decisions quickly or do you like to take your time?

COMMUNICATION

13 Are you good at explaining things to other people?

14 Do you find it embarrassing to talk to people you don't know?

15 At school, do you prefer working in a group or on your own?

16 Are you good at encouraging other people to do things?

INTERESTS AND ABILITIES

17 Are you interested in science and technology?

18 Can you imagine working on a space station?

19 Are you involved in any creative activities at school such as drama or music?

20 Are you good at working with numbers or are you more interested in working with words?

7.7 Improve your writing

In this lesson you will...

- write a profile of yourself.

Imagine you're going to live in another city or country for a year. You're going to have an interview at your new school. The headteacher will ask you to talk about yourself, your personality and your achievements at school and outside school. Write a personal profile to prepare for your interview.

1 **Work with a partner. Take turns to ask and answer these questions.**

a What are your favourite subjects?

b What are you good at?

c What activities are you involved in at school?

d Have you had any special responsibilities?

e What are you most proud of?

f What do you do in your free time?

g Is there any particular activity you enjoy doing?

h How would you describe yourself?

i What are your ambitions for the future?

2 **Work with a partner. Read the personal profile on the opposite page.**

a Which sentences answer the questions in Exercise 1?

b Which sentences give extra information?

Language tip

Notice how the student uses the word *quite* in her profile. She uses it to sound modest.

I'm ***quite*** *good at English.*

I'm ***quite*** *a sociable person, but I'm also* ***quite*** *independent.*

3 Now write a draft of your personal profile in preparation for a school interview.

- Have you written about your favourite subjects and what you're good at?
- Have you mentioned activities you're involved in, special responsibilities and what you're most proud of?
- Have you written about what you do in your free time and a particular activity you enjoy?
- Have you described your personality and said what you'd like to do in the future?
- Have you managed to include the word *quite* in your profile?

4 Write a final version of your profile.

I enjoy all my subjects at school but I'm particularly interested in maths, science and languages. I think I'm quite good at English. I've studied it since I was five years old and I've now started to read stories in English. I also try to watch as many English films as I can to try to improve my English.

I'm quite good at music. I play the flute and my parents encourage me to practise every day, which I don't mind doing at all because I love playing the flute. I'm keen on drama too and this year I've been involved in our school play. I played in the orchestra.

Last term, my headteacher asked me to be one of the students to show new students and parents round the school. I was very proud to be asked.

In my free time, I go swimming. My school chose me to take part in an inter-school competition. I was a bit nervous about it, but once I was in the water I was fine. I like spending time with my friends. Some of us go to a riding school at weekends. I enjoy riding because I love horses and I don't mind helping to look after them.

I think I'm quite a sociable person, but I'm also quite independent and hard-working. I don't know what I want to do in the future, but I'd like to go to university. I'd probably study maths or maybe law.

7.8 Project challenge

Project 1: A quiz

You are going to write and do a quiz about jobs.

Step 1: Everyone in the class writes a list of three jobs they would like to do. Keep the lists secret.

Step 2: Work in groups. Discuss the qualities you need to do certain kinds of jobs. For example, someone who works for the emergency services needs to be decisive, patient and organised. Someone who wants to be a lawyer needs to be logical, good with words and not afraid of speaking in front of other people. Look back at the lists of jobs in Lesson 7.1.

Step 3: In your groups, you're going to write ten questions to find out what kind of jobs people should do.

Here are some different types of question you can ask:

- A 'yes/no' question
  Do you enjoy doing outdoor activities? (Yes/No)
- An open question
  What are you good at? Think of school subjects, sports, music …
- A multiple-choice question
  Which of the following statements is true for you?
  I enjoy solving crosswords.
  I'm quite good at crosswords but I don't do many of them.
  I can't stand doing crosswords.

Step 4: Write your questions. (Look back at questions in the quiz in Lesson 7.6 to help you.)

Step 5: Ask the students in another group your questions. Make notes of their answers.

Step 6: Using your notes, decide which jobs would be suitable for the members of the other group.

Step 7: Tell the students in the other group what jobs you think they should do. Did you come up with any that were on the list they wrote at the beginning?

- How did this project help you to practise the language you learned in this unit?
- How did your classmates respond to your quiz questions, and what did they think of the jobs you suggested for them?

Project 2: A presentation

You are going to give a presentation about a role model.

1 Read the profile of Greta Thunberg. Which of the following are given in the text?

a place of birth
b year of birth
c parents' occupations
d likes and dislikes
e achievements at school
f examples of things she's done
g character and personality
h job she would like to do in the future
i a quote from her

GRETA THUNBERG

Greta Thunberg was born in Stockholm, Sweden in 2003. Her mother is an opera singer and her father is an actor. She's a vegetarian and she enjoys riding her bike and reading. At the age of 15 she began protesting outside the Swedish parliament about the need to stop climate change. She inspired teenagers and others across the world to join her protest. She was featured on the cover of *Time* magazine. She's spoken at international conferences and she has spoken to politicians, and governments across the world. She's not afraid of talking to people who are older than her and in positions of power, and she's very determined. In May 2019, her book, *No One is Too Small to Make a Difference*, was published. It is a collection of her speeches.

Greta Thunberg addressing the World Economic Forum about climate change

'I don't want your hope. I don't want you to be hopeful. I want you to panic. I want you to feel the fear I feel every day. And then I want you to act. I want you to act as you would in a crisis. I want you to act as if our house is on fire. Because it is.'

2 You're going to give a short presentation about a role model.

Step 1: Choose someone you consider to be a role model.

Step 2: Research the information you need. Use the headings in Exercise 1 as a guide.

Step 3: Decide what kind of presentation you're going to give.

- a talk?
- use slides?
- use video?

Step 4: Write your presentation using the text about Greta Thunberg as a model.

Step 5: Find pictures to illustrate it.

Step 6: If possible, find a quote that shows why this person is a good role model.

Step 7: Give your presentation.

Step 8: Ask if anyone has questions.

Step 9: Ask the class to give their opinions of your presentation.

- Did you learn anything new when you were doing your research?
- Is there anything you would change in your presentation?

7.9 Autobiography

The Boy Who Harnessed the Wind

William Kamkwamba is from a small village in Malawi, in Africa. When William was 14, the crops on his family's farm failed and the family had no money. William could no longer go to school. However, he could still use the school library. One day a particular book caught his attention.

56

1 Read and listen to the extract from William's book, *The Boy Who Harnessed the Wind*. What does it tell you about William's personality?

2 Work with a partner. Draw a simple diagram of the pinwheel that William and his friends made. Label it.

3 Work in groups. Discuss these questions.

- a The writer of *Using Energy* refers to Archimedes, a Greek mathematician and inventor. Why?
- b William says in line 3 'this book has since changed my life'. What do you think he means?
- c In which two ways does William think a windmill can be useful in his village?

The story continues like this:

With a windmill, we'd finally release ourselves from the troubles of darkness and hunger. A windmill meant more than just power. It was freedom.

"Gilbert, I'm going to build a windmill."

Imagine and write the rest of the conversation between Gilbert and William.

"All I need is a windmill and I can have lights," I said.

"…

Language tip

Use " to show the start of what someone says.

Use " to show the end of what someone says.

Use a comma at the end of the direct speech and before he said / she said etc.

Start a new paragraph for. each new speaker.

What's this? I wondered.

Pulling it out, I saw it was a textbook from America called *Using Energy* – and this book has since changed my life.

The cover featured a long row of windmills, though at the time I had no idea what a *windmill* was. All I saw were tall white towers with three blades spinning like a fan.

"Gilbert," I said, calling him over. "Don't these look like the pinwheels that you, me, and Geoffrey used to make?"

We used to find old plastic water bottles in the trading center. We'd cut the sides into blades like a fan, drive a nail through the lid, then hang it on a stick. The wind would spin the blades. A kids' toy.

"Yah," he said. "You're right. But these things are giant. What are they for?"

"Let's find out."

"Energy is all around you every day," the book said. "Sometimes energy needs to be converted to another form before it is useful to us. How can we convert forms of energy? Read on and you'll see."

I read on.

"Imagine that hostile forces have invaded your town, and defeat seems certain. If you needed a hero to 'save the day', it's unlikely you would go to the nearest university and drag a scientist to the battlefront. Yet, according to legend, it was not a general who saved the Greek city of Syracuse when the Roman fleet attacked it in 214 BC."

It explained how Archimedes used his "Death Ray" – which was really a lot of mirrors – to reflect the sun onto the enemy ships until, one by one, they caught fire and sank. That was an example of how you can use the sun to produce energy.

Just like with the sun, windmills could also be used to generate power.

"People throughout Europe and the Middle East used windmills for pumping water and grinding grain," it said. "When many wind machines are grouped together on wind farms, they can generate as much electricity as a power plant."

It all snapped together. I turned to Gilbert to see if he was reading the same stuff.

...

All I needed was a windmill and I could have lights.

No more smoky lanterns that left us with sore throats and hacking coughs. With a windmill, I could stay awake and read instead of going to bed at seven with the rest of Malawi.

But most important, a windmill could also pump water.

[5] **blade:** the flat wide part of an object that pushes against air or water

[5] **spin:** to turn around quickly

[7] **pinwheel:** a child's toy like a small windmill on a stick

[9] **trading center:** a place where people buy and sell things

[10] **nail:** a thin piece of metal with a sharp end used to join pieces of wood together

[10] **lid:** the top of a container that you can take off

[18] **hostile:** very unfriendly

[18] **defeat:** losing a fight

[20] **battlefront:** the front line of a war between two armies

[21] **fleet:** a group of ships

[25] **sank:** past tense of *to sink*, go down below the surface of the water

[27] **pump:** to make liquid or gas move in a particular direction

[28] **grind:** to make something (coffee, corn, etc.) into small pieces or powder

[28] **grain:** seed from cereal crops used for food

After many attempts and using scrap metal and parts of an old bicycle, William manages to build a wind turbine. A crowd, including a shopkeeper called Kalino, arrives to watch.

57

4 Read and listen to the second extract.

"That's impossible," Kalino said, laughing. He turned to get a reaction from the crowd. "It looks like a radio tower, and what kind of silly toy is that?"

"Well," I said, "just stand back and watch."

…

"Come on," I said. "Don't embarrass me now."

Just then a strong gust flung me backward. The tower began to rock, so much that I wrapped my elbow around a rung just to hang on. Inches above my head, the blades began to buzz like a set of angry propellers. I clutched the bulb, waiting for my miracle.

Then it came: a flicker, a flash, then a burst of bright, magnificent light. My heart nearly exploded.

"Look!" someone shouted. "He's made light!"

"It's true what he said!"

A group of children pushed through the crowd.

"Look how it spins!"

"Let me see!"

I threw my hands into the air and shouted with joy, laughing so hard that I became dizzy. I held the bulb in triumph and addressed the unbelievers:

"Electric wind!" I shouted. "I told you I wasn't mad."

One by one, the people began to cheer. They waved their hands and shouted, "*Wachitabwina*! Well done!"

"You did it, William!"

"That's right," I said, "And now I'm going bigger! Just wait and see!"

[4] **embarrass:** make someone feel anxious or uncomfortable

[5] **gust:** a sudden strong wind

[5] **flung:** past tense of *fling*, throw someone or something suddenly and with force

[5] **backward:** towards the direction behind you

[6] **rung:** one of the bars that forms the steps of a ladder

[7] **clutch:** hold something tightly

[9] **flicker:** a light that goes on and off

[9] **flash:** a bright light that shines for a short time

[9] **burst of light:** a sudden increase in light

[17] **dizzy:** feeling as if you or the things around you are spinning

5 In 2019, William's story was made into a film. Write the scene for the second extract.

- Start at the point where the crowd gathers.
- Include what Kalino and others say.
- You can add other reactions and comments.
- Then move to the point where the blades start to turn.
- Include what people say and add other reactions and comments.
- Act out the scene.

Check your progress

General knowledge quiz

How much can you remember about what you have learned?

1 What do you call someone who prepares medicine for people but is not a doctor?

2 What do you call someone who designs buildings?

3 What do you call someone who acts for you in a court of law?

4 What do the letters IT stand for in relation to areas of work?

5 What is this person's job?

6 Name two other jobs in the emergency services.

7 In which continent are Ethiopia and Malawi?

8 What does a hydroelectric generator do?

9 What is a prototype?

10 The British Racing School in Newmarket, a town in Britain, is associated with which sport: motor racing, horse racing or cycling?

Vocabulary

Jobs

1 **Complete the sentences.**

a I've got a problem with my teeth. Do you know a good ***dentist***?

b Our neighbour knows a lot about cars. He's a ……… .

c I like cooking but I don't want to work as a ……… .

d Oh no! I think the water pipe has burst. Call the ……… .

e I'd like to fly a plane. How do you become a ……… ?

Personality

2 **Choose the correct adjective.**

adventurous	modest
determined	optimistic
easy-going	

This word describes someone who …

a does not talk about how good they are.

b is usually relaxed and calm, not worried or upset.

c does not give up trying until they have achieved their aim.

d always thinks that good things will happen.

e likes to try new or difficult things.

Use of English

1 Complete the sentences with the correct preposition.

a My younger brother is full .... energy.

b We were all worried .... the test.

c Are you interested .... cricket?

d Your jacket is similar .... mine.

2 Use one of the adjectives below followed by *to* to complete each sentence.

nice	easy	pleased
surprised		

a I'm ***pleased to*** meet you.

b I'm .... hear that you didn't win the technology prize.

c Don't worry, it's .... make a mistake.

d It's .... know that they're happy.

3 Choose the correct option.

a Don't forget *to send / sending* me a message.

b I feel like *to watch / watching* a film this evening.

c She loves riding and hopes *to be / being* a successful jockey.

d We have decided *to have / having* a barbecue at the weekend.

4 Put the words in the correct order.

a always / encouraged / have / independent / me / My parents / to be

b Does / expect / in the house / to help her / you / your mother / ?

c advises / every day / Our teacher / some vocabulary / to learn / us

d Maths homework / asked / I / her / me / to help / with my

Summary checklist

I can

- ☐ describe what people do in their jobs.
- ☐ read and talk about how science can improve people's lives.
- ☐ understand people talking about the difficulties they face in everyday life.
- ☐ use adjectives to describe personality (*easy-going, decisive*).
- ☐ talk about what sort of job I would like and the ambitions I have.
- ☐ discuss what makes a good role model.
- ☐ ask and answer questions about my interests, personal strengths and skills.
- ☐ write a profile of myself to prepare for an interview at a new school.
- ☐ write questions for a quiz on jobs.
- ☐ give a presentation about a role model.

8 In the news

In this unit you will…

- **listen** to and talk about what's in a school magazine
- **learn** about the early history of news
- **read** news stories and decide whether they are true or false
- **learn** and **use** expressions connected with social media
- **compare** the information in three newspaper reports
- **identify** implied meaning in a newspaper article
- **write** a newspaper report.

Getting started

"What's in the news at the moment?"

Watch this!

8.1 A school magazine

In this lesson you will...

- listen to and talk about what's in a school magazine
- use the present perfect for events in the recent past.

- **What do you expect to find in a school magazine?**

Listen

58 **1** **Who is talking to the radio presenter? What are they talking about?**

2 **Answer the questions.**

a How many issues are there per year?
b Who writes the magazine?
c There are several sections in the magazine. Can you give an example of one or two of them?
d Who is Mrs Gifford and what does she do?
e Is the magazine available in print and online?

Writing tip

For Exercise 3 you need to take notes as you listen. Only write down key words. Don't write whole sentences.

59 **3** **Copy the headings from the school magazine and listen to the next part of the interview. For each heading give an example from the summer issue.**

Hillfield School Magazine

Editor: Mrs Gifford

Events
News in brief
Sports
Puzzles
Stories and features

Remember Present perfect to talk about events in the recent past

For something that has happened very recently, use *just* with the present perfect.

I've just written *a report on the inter-school basketball tournament.*

4 Complete the second sentence in each of these pairs of sentences.

a Jasmine did a test on Monday, a test on Tuesday and a test on Wednesday.
Jasmine ***'s done*** three tests this week.

b I finished my story for the magazine five minutes ago.
I ……… just ……… my story for the magazine.

c I wrote the clues for the crossword last night.
I ……… ……… the clues for the crossword.

d The English teachers did the questionnaire about holidays this morning.
The English teachers ……… just ……… the questionnaire about holidays.

5 Work with a partner. Write four sentences about things that have happened and things that you've learned about at school this week. Can you include anything that has just happened?

This week, we've had a test in maths and a test in geography.
We've just had a talk on first aid, so we've learned about how to deal with minor injuries.

Speaking

6 Work in groups. Discuss what to write for each section of a school magazine. Think of things that have happened recently. Write notes and keep them. You will need them later in this unit.

Inter-school football match – score 3:3
Visit to local fire station
Year 8 concert

8.2 What's in the news?

In this lesson you will...

- learn about the early history of news
- discuss how news reporting has changed.

Key words: Media studies

adverts
copies (of a newspaper)
daily newspaper
reports

- **What do you expect to read in a national newspaper?**

Reading

1 **Read the text. How are newspapers today different? Use the words in the media studies key words box to help you.**

The early history of news

Acta Diurna

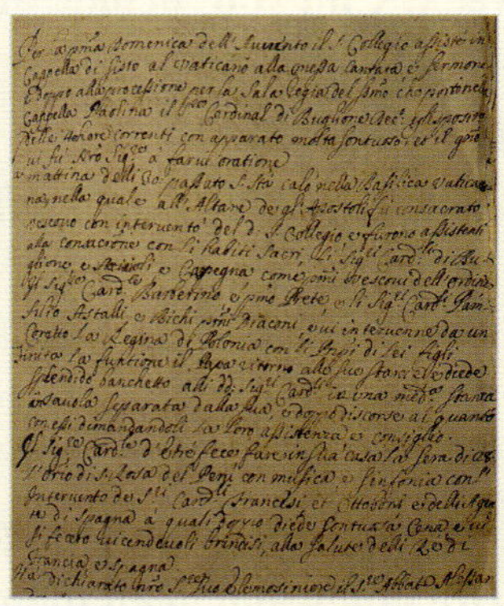

Avvisi

The first printed news sheets were produced in Germany

The second issue of the world's first daily newspaper

In Ancient Rome, the *Acta Diurna* contained reports of daily events, such as marriages, deaths and the results of trials in court. They were carved in stone and were put up in public places so that everyone could read them. Historians think that they date from before 59 BCE and were started by Emperor Julius Caesar.

Handwritten news sheets, called *avvisi*, were circulated in Rome and in Venice in the 16th century. Powerful people decided what could appear in them. They contained political, military and economic news and were single sheets of paper, folded to make four pages and issued weekly. As they were handwritten, not many copies were produced. However, the news they contained was spread quickly by word of mouth.

The first printed news sheets appeared in Germany in 1609. They were censored by the government. Therefore, they only contained foreign news. There was no home news.

The world's first daily newspaper, the *Daily Courant*, was published on 11 March 1702 by Elizabeth Mallet in London. It was a single page with news on one side and adverts on the other side. She said that she was only going to publish foreign news and that she would not add any comments of her own as she thought her readers had 'sense enough to make reflections for themselves'.

2 Find words in the text that mean the following.

- **a** the process of making a decision in court about whether someone is guilty of a crime
- **b** cut (into a hard material)
- **c** passed round from one person to another
- **d** relating to the army
- **e** only one
- **f** controlled (in terms of content)

3 Find these two expressions in the text. What do they mean?

- **a** 'the news was spread by word of mouth'
- **b** 'the readers had sense enough to make reflections for themselves'

> **Use of English** Connectives:
> *because, so that, as, therefore, however, although*
>
> Use connectives to link parts of a sentence.
> Use **however** and **therefore** to link two separate sentences.
>
> **Find examples in the text on the opposite page.**

4 Complete the sentences with a connective.

- **a** I usually read news online ……….. I don't want to buy a newspaper.
- **b** Not everything you read online is true. ……….., you have to check information carefully.
- **c** I enjoy writing. ……….., I don't want to be a journalist.
- **d** We publish the magazine online, ……….. some people still request a printed version.
- **e** ……….. there is a lot of work to do on the magazine, we have a big team of reporters.

Speaking

5 Work in groups. Discuss the questions. Give your opinions.

- **a** Why do you think Julius Caesar believed it was a good idea to publish the *Acta Diurna*?
- **b** How do you think the *avvisi* could be useful to powerful people?
- **c** Why do you think the German government didn't want the news sheets to cover home news?
- **d** Why do you think the *Daily Courant* had adverts as well as news?
- **e** Why do you think printed newspapers are less popular now?
- **f** What should a newspaper today give you?

8.3 Can it be true?

In this lesson you will...

- read news stories and decide whether they are true or false.

- **Have you ever heard or read anything that seemed unbelievable at first but was in fact true?**

Reading

1 **Read these two news items. Which do you think has the best headline? Give reasons for your answer.**

News > World > Australasia

Australia to impose 24-hour curfew on all cats to protect endangered species

Siobhan Fenton | @siobhanfenton
53 comments

Australian cat owners could have to keep their pets indoors permanently under a '24-hour cat curfew' proposed by the government.

The proposal has been made by Australia's first 'threatened species commissioner', Gregory Andrews, in a bid to protect native animals facing extinction due to cat attacks, according to the *The Sydney Morning Herald*.

Slide into class

A school in Toronto, Canada, with just under 1200 students, has introduced a new way of getting around. Rather than using the narrow stairs that lead from one floor to another, students and teachers now move quickly and easily between classrooms using slides – the sort you might find in a children's playground. The school council at Highbury Grove, which consists of teachers, parents and students, decided that replacing the stairs with slides would help students get to lessons on time. In the past, students were often late because the stairs were so crowded, but that no longer happens. The experiment has proved to be a great success, and also great fun.

2 Read the two news items again. Answer these questions.

News item 1

- a Does *permanently* mean 'some of the time' or 'all of the time'?
- b What is a *curfew*?
- c What is Gregory Andrews's job?
- d What is Gregory Andrews trying to do?
- e What is *The Sydney Morning Herald*?

News item 2

- f What is Highbury Grove and where is it?
- g What has changed at Highbury Grove?
- h Are there more or fewer than 1200 students at Highbury Grove?
- i Who decided to make this change: the students, the teachers or the parents?
- j What was the reason for the change?

Listening and speaking

60 **3 Listen to two people discussing the first news item. Do they agree with each other?**

61 **4 Listen to two people discussing the second news item. How would you summarise their views?**

5 Work in small groups. Discuss the news items. Are they both true? Are they both false? Or is one true and one false?

Use these phrases in your discussion.

Have you read this story about …?
What did you think?

I think it could be true.
It sounds like a good idea to me.

It can't be true.
It sounds strange to me.
You can't believe everything you read.
It sounds a bit unlikely to me.
No, I don't believe it.

62 **6 Real news or fake news? Listen and find out.**

8.4 A human interest story

In this lesson you will…

- learn and use expressions connected with social media
- use quantifiers to compare people (*both*, *each other*, *either*, *neither*).

- **What are the advantages and disadvantages of being a twin?**

Reading

1 **This story appeared in an online newspaper. Why do you think it made the news?**

> Identical twin sisters, separated at birth and brought up 4000 miles apart, describe the moment they discovered each other on social media.

63

2 **Listen to a story about two girls, Anaïs Bordier and Samantha Futerman. Answer these questions.**

a What four things do they have in common?

b In their video call, what do you think they asked each other?

c How do you think this story continues?

3 **Use the phrases in the box to summarise the story so far.**

send someone a video link	contact someone via social media
click on a link	send a friend request
find out about someone or something	accept a request
type something into your phone	become friends on social media
google someone or something	have a video conversation

4 **Read how the story ended. Did it end as you expected?**

One year and one DNA test later, they knew that they were twin sisters who had been separated at birth. Both Anaïs and Samantha speak English, although French is Anaïs's first language. The girls say they both felt that something was missing in their lives but now that they have found each other, they have extra confidence.

Neither the Futermans nor the Bordier family knew that the baby they had adopted was a twin. Mrs Futerman said, 'We would have taken both of you'.

When Anaïs and Samantha met for the first time in London, they realised just how much they had in common. Both of them are interested in the arts, they have the same favourite TV programmes, they both hate cooked carrots and neither of them likes getting up early.

Has either of them ever pretended to be the other one? They're not saying ...

Use of English Quantifiers: *both (of), each other / one another, either of / neither of*

both

Use *both* to talk about two people (or things) together.

Both *Anaïs and Samantha speak English.*

both of

Use *both of* before the object pronouns *us*, *you*, *them*.

Both of *them are interested in the arts.*

each other / one another

Each other and *one another* mean the same.

They got in touch with ***one another****.*

either of / neither of

Use *either* when you mean 'one or the other'.

Has ***either of*** *them ever pretended to be the other one?*

Use *neither* when you mean 'not one and not the other'.

Neither of *them likes getting up early.*

We usually use *either* and *neither* with a singular verb.

5 Complete the sentences using *both*, *both of*, *each other*, *either of*, or *neither of*.

a Anaïs and Samantha were .... adopted.

b .... them were born in Busan, in South Korea.

c .... them knew they were twins until they made contact.

d When they talked, they asked .... a lot of questions.

e Has .... them appeared in films? Yes, Samantha has.

Speaking

6 Find someone in the class who is similar to you. Ask questions such as:

a What's your favourite food?

b What are you interested in? What do you do in your free time?

c What don't you like? (*getting up early, kinds of food, music, …*)

d How long have we known each other?

8.5 What are the facts?

In this lesson you will...

- understand information in a newspaper article
- use complex noun phrases.

Key words: Maths

Fractions	How to say it
$\frac{1}{2}$	'half'
$\frac{3}{4}$	'three quarters'
Decimals and percentages	**How to say it**
14.23%	'fourteen point two three per cent'

Use the preposition *of* after these expressions, for example *more than 95% of British teenagers.*

- **What are the rules about mobile phones in your school?**

Reading

1 **Read this newspaper article. Why is this topic in the news?**

The Newhaven Gazette

Mobile phones in schools

From our Education correspondent

A recently published report has caused schools to rethink their policies on mobile phones.

Researchers from the London School of Economics looked at 91 schools in four British cities (Birmingham, Leicester, London and Manchester). Their 12-year study found that exam results went up by an average of 6.4% after mobiles were banned from the classroom. Students who usually achieved low marks benefited most from the ban, with exam marks increasing by 14.23%, although the marks of high-achieving students were not significantly different.

More than 95% of British teenagers take a mobile to school. After reading the report, some schools said they are considering asking students to hand in their phones to the school office before going into class, so that they are not distracted by them.

However, some parents are unhappy about this, because their children might need to get in touch with them during the day. Some teachers have also said that mobiles can be useful in class – for example, if a student wants to look up the meaning of a word.

All schools in Newhaven have a mobile phone policy, although over half of them said they had difficulty enforcing it.

2 **Match the words from the text with their definitions.**

1	to rethink	a	getting good results
2	to ban	b	in an important or big way
3	to achieve	c	to be helped by something
4	to benefit	d	to contact
5	high-achieving	e	to have your attention taken away from something
6	significantly	f	to make people obey a rule or a law
7	to be distracted	g	to stop people from using or doing something
8	to get in touch with	h	to succeed in doing something
9	to enforce	i	to think again

Use of English Complex noun phrases

simple noun
A report *was published recently. It has caused schools to rethink their policies on mobile phones.*

complex noun phrase
A recently published report *has caused schools to rethink their policy on phones.*

simple noun
Researchers *looked at 91 schools. The researchers were from the London School of Economics.*

complex noun phrase
Researchers from the London School of Economics *looked at 91 schools.*

Find sentences in the text that use complex noun phrases to give the information in the following sentences.

- Researchers looked at 91 schools. The schools were in four British cities.
- Their study found that students' exam results improved by 6.4%. It lasted twelve years.

3 **Look at these pairs of sentences. Use complex noun phrases to rewrite them as one sentence.**

a This phone charger is good but it's quite expensive. It's solar-powered.
*This **solar-powered phone charger is good but quite expensive**.*

b There's a shop that sells mobiles. It's next to the newsagents.
The shop …

c The instructions tell you all you need to know. They are on the back of the packet.
The …

d Our maths teacher has an app. It's used for setting homework.
Our maths teacher has an app …

4 **Answer these questions.**

a Who wrote the report?

b What was the main conclusion of the report?

c Why might a ban on mobile phones be good for low-achieving students?

d How might the report change the mobile phone policy of some schools?

e Do you agree with the reactions of some parents and teachers to the ban?

8.6 A dramatic event

In this lesson you will...

- identify implied meaning in a newspaper article
- use the past continuous to describe a dramatic event (*Ben was snowboarding ...*).

- **Snowboarding and skiing in the mountains can be great fun but there are risks, such as avalanches. What is an avalanche? What other risks are there?**

Reading

1 Read the article. Why is the title 'Saved by his phone'?

Saved by his phone

A snowboarder was feeling lucky to be alive yesterday after a dramatic helicopter rescue.

Ben Akintola, 30, was snowboarding in the French Alps under a clear blue sky when an avalanche started. He didn't have time to escape. It hit him with full force and knocked him unconscious.

He woke in the middle of the night in pitch darkness. He was lying on a narrow, icy ledge. Amazingly, he still had a phone signal, so he called a friend a thousand kilometres away in Britain. His friend called the French rescue services.

'I was waiting for what seemed like hours on that narrow ledge,' said Ben. 'I was beginning to give up hope when I heard the sound of a helicopter. It was circling around in the darkness, looking for me. I was waving my phone around desperately. Fortunately, the helicopter pilot saw the light. I was overjoyed when the helicopter headed my way. It hovered above me and began lowering a rope.'

Ben was in hospital last night, but his doctor said he did not have any serious injuries. He's looking forward to going home today.

The French rescue services said: 'We were very pleased that we were able to rescue Ben. The risk of avalanches off-piste is much higher at this time of year. All snowboarders and skiers should stay on the ski runs and not go off-piste. Ben had a lucky escape.'

[5] **with full force:** very hard, with a lot of strength

[5] **unconscious:** not able to see, feel, move, etc.

[6] **pitch darkness:** completely without light

[7] **ledge:** a narrow, flat area on the side of a mountain

[13] **desperately:** needing or wanting something very much

[14] **overjoyed:** very happy

[14] **to hover:** to stay in the same position in the air

2 Read the newspaper article. The following statements are implied in the text. Give reasons for saying that we know they are true.

- a Ben was unconscious for several hours.
  This is implied because we know that the avalanche happened during the day, when the sky was blue. But Ben woke in the middle of the night.
- b It's not always easy to get a phone signal in the mountains.
- c Ben didn't know the number of the French rescue services.
- d Ben used the torch on his phone to attract the pilot's attention.
- e Ben was snowboarding off-piste.
- f The French rescue services thought that Ben put himself in danger by snowboarding on his own.

Reading tip

A writer doesn't always state things directly. Sometimes meaning is 'implied': the writer suggests something is true or that something happened, without actually saying it.

Use of English Past continuous

Look at this sentence:

He woke in the middle of the night in pitch darkness.

past tense of *be* verb + *-ing*

*He **was lying** on a narrow, icy ledge.*

How do you use the past continuous and when do you use it?

- The past continuous is often used in narrative descriptions:

  *A snowboarder **was feeling** lucky to be alive yesterday after a dramatic helicopter rescue.*
- We can also use the past continuous and the past simple together to show that one action interrupted another: *He **was snowboarding** in the French Alps under a clear blue sky **when an avalanche started**.*

How many more examples of the past continuous can you find in the newspaper story?

Speaking

3 Role-play an interview between a TV news journalist and Ben after he left hospital. Here are some questions the journalist can ask. Remember to use the past continuous when necessary in your answers.

- a Ben, tell me, where were you and what were you doing?
- b What was the weather like? Was it snowing?
- c What happened?
- d Where were you when you woke up?
- e What did you do next?

8.7 Improve your writing

In this lesson you will...

- write a newspaper report.

You're going to write a newspaper report of a dramatic rescue.

Step 1: On the opposite page, you will see some notes either side of the story, 'Saved by his phone'. Read them. The notes will help you when you write your own report.

Step 2: Here is an idea for a story about a dramatic rescue. Work in pairs. Look at the pictures and describe what happened.

SAVED BY A MAP AND A MOBILE

Eighteen-year-old Lara Moore had a lucky escape yesterday.

Step 3: Ask and answer the questions – the '5 Ws + how': *Who?*, *What?*, *When?*, *Where?*, *Why?* and *How?*.

Step 4: Write down as many facts as possible about the story.

Step 5: Plan your report in order to make a good story. Follow the plan of the story 'Saved by his phone'.

Step 6: **Write a draft of your story. Ask other students to comment on it.**

Step 7:

- Have you found a good headline for your story?
- Does the first sentence give a short clear summary of the story?
- Have you used both the past continuous and the past simple?
- Have you used quotes in speech marks (' ') to make your story more interesting?
- Does your story answer the '5Ws + How'?

Step 8: **Write the final version of your story.**

The headline (title) needs to capture the reader's attention.

The first sentence should give a short, clear summary of the story.

Use the past continuous to set the scene and the past simple to talk about events.

If you use quotes to make your report more interesting, don't forget to use speech marks.

Saved by his phone

A snowboarder was feeling lucky to be alive yesterday after a dramatic helicopter rescue.

Ben Akintola, 30, was snowboarding in the French Alps under a clear blue sky when an avalanche started. He didn't have time to escape. It hit him with full force and knocked him unconscious.

He woke in the middle of the night in pitch darkness. He was lying on a narrow, icy ledge. Amazingly, he still had a phone signal, so he called a friend a thousand kilometres away in Britain. His friend called the French rescue services.

'I was waiting for what seemed like hours on that narrow ledge,' said Ben. 'I was beginning to give up hope when I heard the sound of a helicopter. It was circling around in the darkness, looking for me. I was waving my phone around desperately. Fortunately, the helicopter pilot saw the light. I was overjoyed when the helicopter headed my way. It hovered above me and began lowering a rope.'

Ben was in hospital last night but his doctor said he did not have any serious injuries. He's looking forward to going home today.

The French rescue services said: 'We were very pleased that we were able to rescue Ben. The risk of avalanches off-piste is much higher at this time of year. All snowboarders and skiers should stay on the ski runs and not go off-piste. Ben had a lucky escape.'

Who is the story about?

Where was he?

What happened?

When did it happen?

How was he rescued?

Why did it happen?

8.8 Project challenge

Project 1: News and puzzles sections of a school magazine

You're going to plan and write an issue of a magazine for your school using Project 1 and Project 2.

Section A: News

Work in pairs. You are in charge of the 'news in brief' section. You're going to write short news items about what's happened this term. Each item is only two or three sentences long. Look at the example to help you.

> **News in brief**
>
> We've had several interesting visitors this term …
>
> In March, the TV news presenter Elif Balcan came to talk to us. She was a student at this school. She told us about her career in journalism and news reporting.
>
> We've also welcomed the well-known author, Soniah Kamal, who gave a very amusing talk about living and writing in different countries.

Section B: Puzzles

Work in pairs. You are in charge of the puzzles section. Puzzles can be crosswords, word searches, picture puzzles, etc. You can also include jokes and cartoons. Look at the example to help you.

Word wheel

How many words can you make using the letters in the word wheel? You can use the letter in the centre of the wheel more than once, but you can only use the other letters once.

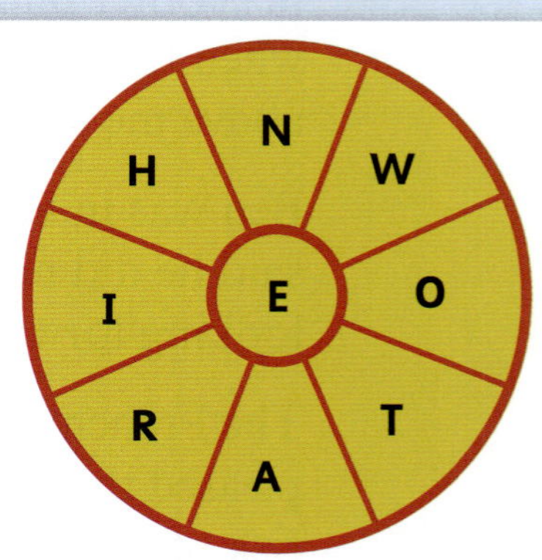

Share ideas in your group and decide what you're going to write about.

- www – What went well?
- ebi – Even better if …

Project 2: Events and sports sections of a school magazine

You're going to plan and write an issue of a magazine for your school using Project 1 and Project 2.

Section C: Events

Work in groups, You're in charge of the events section. You're going to write about major events this term such as concerts, celebrations and school trips. Follow the steps below.

Section D: Sports

Work in groups. You're in charge of the sports section. You're going to write about sports events this term such as football matches and athletics competitions. Follow the steps below.

Step 1: Plan what you want to write about.

Step 2: Divide the work among the members of your group.

We've just had the school play. Who's interested in writing about that?

You're keen on sports. Why don't you write about the basketball match?

Step 3: Write a draft of your article. Ask other students to read it and make suggestions for improvements. Are the ideas clearly expressed? Can you improve what you've written by including connectives such as *although, so that, however*, etc.?

Step 4: Choose photos or illustrations for your articles and write captions for them.

Step 5: Check your article for spelling, grammar and punctuation.

Step 6: Write the final version.

Sports day: the winner of the 400-metre race

- What was the most difficult thing about writing pieces for the school magazine?
- What did you like about what other people wrote?

8.9 Autobiography

Separated @ Birth

Separated @ Birth is a book written by Anaïs Bordier and Samantha Futerman. You read about them in Lesson 8.4. Anaïs wrote Chapter 1, Samantha wrote Chapter 2, and so on.

64

1 Read and listen to this extract from Chapter 7. Why do you think Anaïs at first tried to ignore the idea of a video conversation with Samantha?

7 ANAÏS

first skype call with samantha

Discovering a person through social media is insane. There were pictures and snippets of dialogue, but there was not yet common ground. Our histories up until this point had been completely separate, and all of a sudden, we were becoming spontaneous best friends, only on a hunch that we might be twins separated at birth. I found it somewhat difficult to think of topics to bring up during our messaging sessions – after all, she was someone I knew absolutely nothing about, but with whom I felt identical.

Messaging each other definitely was the best first approach: first, I wasn't self-conscious and felt protected in the anonymity of typing as opposed to face-to-face communication; and second, I could think longer about what I was going to put down on paper, or should I say, type on the keyboard. I even had time to review and edit anything I said, in case it sounded weird or wrong. On the other hand, writing can be very puzzling as people express themselves differently with their choice of words, and therefore a written message can still be misunderstood in the nuances. Further complicating matters was that English was my second language, making it even more nerve-wracking.

Those first few days, Samantha and I kept things fun and general. I told her I was an only child, I was in my final year of design school, and I liked to go to bed late, so she needn't worry about the eight-hour time difference between us.

[1] **insane:** mad
[2] **snippet:** a small piece
[2] **common ground:** things we both knew about
[4] **all of a sudden:** suddenly
[4] **spontaneous:** not planned or organised
[5] **hunch:** an idea that something is true
[6] **bring up:** to mention
[10] **self-conscious:** worried about what other people think of you
[10] **anonymity:** when other people don't know who you are or what your name is
[14] **weird:** very strange
[17] **nuance:** very small difference in meaning
[18] **complicate matters:** to make things more difficult than necessary
[19] **nerve-wracking:** making you very nervous

> The idea of "seeing" Samantha in a Skype call was floating somewhere in my field of neurons, but I guess I was trying to ignore it.

[24] **float:** to move gently through the air

[25] **neuron:** a nerve cell that carries messages between your brain and other parts of your body

2 Values Discuss these questions.

a. Was it a good idea for Anaïs and Samantha to write alternate chapters of the book? Give reasons for your answer.

b. Why does Anaïs say that 'discovering a person through social media is insane'?

c. Anaïs mentions two advantages and two disadvantages of messaging. Do you agree with what she says?

Anaïs and Samantha agree to talk to each other on Skype. The next extract describes the moment they see each other on screen.

> Something was coming into focus on my screen. I SEE MYSELF PIXELISED! It was unbelievable. It was me, but wearing a white lacy blouse with short sleeves! Even pixelated, we look so identical. Wait, she is moving. Wait, she looks so nice. She is smiling. She looks happy. Oh, she is giggling. And so am I. I can't believe it. This is really it. We are reunited!
>
> ...
>
> The first few minutes of the call were surreal. I felt like I was floating on a cloud, like time had frozen around me, around us. Time and space did not matter any more, because we were on opposite sides of the earth, talking at the same time. In the first moments, we were even talking in different languages. When Samantha asked me, "How's it going?" I answered in French! "Ça va" came out without me even thinking about it. "This is a really weird experience," I said.

[2] **pixelised, pixelated:** made up of pixels (the smallest unit of an image on a screen)

[5] **giggle:** to laugh in an excited way that is difficult to control

3 Answer these questions about the style of the second extract.

a. Why does Anaïs use a lot of short sentences in the first paragraph of this extract?

b. Does she only use the past simple tense? Which other tenses does she use, and why?

c. Which words and devices does she use to express her excitement?

d. Anaïs describes the first minutes of the call as 'surreal' – so strange that she couldn't believe it was real. What examples does she give of this feeling?

4 **Read and listen about the first time the girls met. Then answer the questions.**

66

12 SAM

coming face-to-face with … myself

I sat just staring at the door, waiting to see who was about to enter. And then, I started to squeal as an Asian girl came quickly running through the door. Ahh, oh, right, it wasn't Anaïs. It was her friend Jennifer. I burst into laughter and gave her a massive hug. I had seen her on Instagram, but I didn't know that she was coming with Anaïs. As I turned around again, the sweetest face popped into the doorway and walked hesitantly into the room. Her face was mine, but it was bright red, and her hair was a mess. I froze. And then, I had the longest and most uncomfortable laughing fit I've ever had in my life. I couldn't stop. My brain wasn't working. My body was just pumping blood and adrenaline all the way through. I was hot, sweating, freezing, and amped up all at the same time. It was me … it was me … she was me!

[1] **stare:** to look at someone or something directly for a long time
[2] **squeal:** to make a loud, high sound because you're afraid or excited
[6] **pop:** to appear suddenly
[7] **hesitantly:** slowly, pausing because you're not sure
[8] **froze:** past tense of to freeze, (here) standing completely still
[9] **fit:** a strong, sudden physical reaction you can't control
[11] **adrenaline:** the substance your body produces when you are angry, excited or frightened
[12] **amped up:** showing great excitement or nervousness

a How does Samantha react when she finally meets Anaïs? Can you explain her reaction?

b At the end of the extract, Sam says, 'It was me … it was me … she was me!' Can you explain what she means?

c Authors sometimes write a dedication at the beginning of a book, to thank people or to say who the book is for. This is the dedication Anaïs and Samantha wrote at the beginning of their book. Why do you think they wrote it?

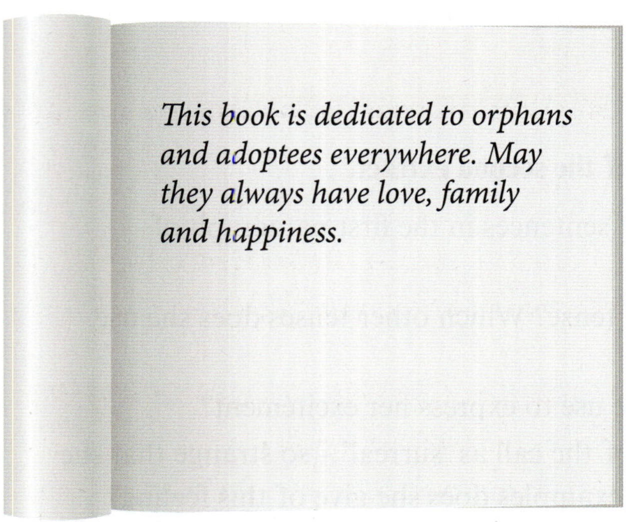
This book is dedicated to orphans and adoptees everywhere. May they always have love, family and happiness.

Check your progress

General knowledge quiz

How much can you remember about what you have learned?

1 Who was Julius Caesar?

2 This is an example of the *Acta Diurna*.

What could you read about in the *Acta Diurna*?

3 What were the *Acta Diurna* written on?

4 *Avvisi* were circulated in Venice in the 16th century. What were they?

5 In which country were the first news sheets printed?

6 In which century was the world's first daily newspaper published and in which language was it written?

7 The first daily newspaper, the *Daily Courant*, was a single sheet with news on one side. What was on the other side?

8 What is *The Sydney Morning Herald*?

9 What are the Alps and what are two sports you can do there in winter?

10 Which vehicle is used in an air rescue in mountainous areas?

Vocabulary

News

1 **Complete the words.**

a The person who is responsible for the content of a magazine or newspaper is called the ed...........

b The people who write the news for newspapers are called re...........

c A crossword is a kind of word pu...........

d The school magazine has three is........... per year.

e There's an online version and a pr........... version.

Media

2 **Complete the sentences with a verb from the box in the correct form.**

accept contact send type watch

a I've found a great story for our magazine. Shall I .... you the link to it?

b Just .... the answer in the box.

c My sister found out how to mend her bike by .... a video.

d I don't know his address but you can .... him via social media.

e You have to be very careful about .... a request to be friends on social media.

Use of English

1 Choose the correct option in each case.

My friend and I are quite similar. We've known *one another / both*[a] since we were 5 years old. *Both of / Either of*[b] us like sports clothes but *either of / neither of*[c] us likes shopping. It's quite funny because sometimes when we see *both of us / each other*[d] at the weekend, we're wearing identical T-shirts. One thing you can be sure of is that you'll never see *either of / both of*[e] us in a suit and tie because we don't like formal clothes.

2 Complete the newspaper story using the verbs in the box in the past continuous.

climb come make push sit try

Cat hero saves life of owner

Last Saturday, at 2.30 in the morning, Melvin Cooper woke up suddenly because his cat, Cassie, ***was sitting*** on his pillow. Cassie ....[a] a lot of noise and she ....[b] her head against Melvin's. Puzzled, Melvin put her on the floor. He ....[c] to get back to sleep when Cassie jumped up again. Melvin picked her up, took her to the bedroom door and opened it. To his horror, he saw that smoke ....[d] up the stairs. Cassie ran back into the bedroom and jumped onto the window ledge. Melvin followed. Melvin and Cassie ....[e] out of the bedroom window onto the garage roof when the firefighters arrived.

Summary checklist

I can

- ☐ talk about what's in a school magazine.
- ☐ discuss the purpose of newspapers in the past and today.
- ☐ read news stories and decide whether they are true or false.
- ☐ use expressions connected with social media.
- ☐ compare the information in newspaper reports.
- ☐ discuss reasons for and against banning mobile phones in schools.
- ☐ identify implied meaning in a newspaper article.
- ☐ role-play an interview between a TV news journalist and someone who had a lucky escape.
- ☐ write a newspaper report about a dramatic event.
- ☐ plan and write an issue of a school magazine.

9 The digital world

In this unit you will...

- **use** reported speech: statements and questions
- **read** an article about an unusual restaurant
- **ask** and **answer** questions in a survey
- **give** exact, detailed instructions in a logical order
- **find** out about technology in farming
- **listen** to someone talking about a challenge
- **give** a presentation about the advantages of using digital devices.

Getting started

“How does technology help us in our everyday life?”

Watch this!

9.1 Keeping in touch

In this lesson you will...

- use reported speech: statements and questions
- learn words and expressions for digital communication.

- **How do you keep in touch with your family and friends?**

Vocabulary

1 Match each sentence to a symbol.

a I've just **downloaded** a really useful app.
b You don't need to type in a password. You just use **Touch ID**.
c What's the **Wi-Fi** code?
d **Voice recognition** is useful for people who find it difficult to use a keyboard.
e Have you **uploaded** your holiday photos yet?
f My friend always uses a lot of **emojis** in her texts.
g I'll add you to my **contacts** list.

1 
2 
3 
4 
5 
6 
7 

Listening

67 **2 Listen to the radio interview with Professor Anderson. What is she talking about?**

Remember Reported statements

Young people can keep in touch with each other much more easily.

*She said (that) people **could** keep in touch with each other much more easily.*

It's an important social skill.

*She said it **was** an important social skill.*

Students don't have to buy expensive books.

*She said (that) students **didn't** have to buy expensive books.*

Remember to change the pronouns.

That worries me.

*She said that worried **her**.*

3 **Listen again and answer the questions.**

a According to the professor, why is digital communication not always meaningful communication?

b What does she say about using information taken directly from the internet for homework?

c What are the professor's views on young people's writing skills?

Use of English Reported questions and requests

To report questions that begin with a question word, change the tense and leave out *do / does / did*.

Presenter: What do you mean?

The *presenter asked the professor what she* ***meant***.

To report *yes / no* questions, use *if*, change the tense and leave out *do / does / did*.

Presenter: Do you think young people are writing more?

The presenter asked the professor ***if*** she ***thought*** young people were writing more.

To report a request or a command, use *ask / tell* someone to do something.

Presenter: Please stay to answer some of the listeners' questions.

The presenter ***asked*** the professor ***to stay*** to answer some of the listeners' questions.

68 4 **Work with a partner. Listen to what listeners said when they phoned in to the radio programme. Take turns to tell each other what they said.**

A: *He said that people spent too much time looking at their phones.*

B: *She said …*

Speaking

5 **Work with a partner. Ask and answer.**

Partner A:

Which apps do you enjoy using?

Do you play games on your phone?

How do you contact your friends when you're on holiday?

Please show me how to do a screenshot.

Partner B:

Do you use the internet to help you with your homework?

How do you listen to music?

Do you watch films on your phone?

Send me the link to the school website, please.

6 **Work with a different partner. Tell him / her the questions you were asked and say what your response was.**

She asked me which apps I enjoyed using. I said I enjoyed using a maths app and a puzzles app.

9.2 A restaurant with a difference

In this lesson you will...

- read an article about an unusual restaurant
- use words and expressions to do with technology.

Key words: Technology

built-in facial recognition technology
digital tablet
humanoid
malfunction
robot
to charge

- **Look at the picture in the article. What does it show?**

Reading

1 **Read the article. What is the attraction of this restaurant in India?**

2 **Look at the terms in the technology key words box. Find them in the article. What are they in your language?**

3 **Write the questions for these answers, based on the information in the text.**

a 18 August ***When did the Robot Restaurant open?***
b An average of five to six hundred.
c Indo-Asian.
d You use a digital tablet.
e So that the robots can move around easily.
f Arya, Ramya, Zoey, Alice and Sansa.
g China.
h In Saudi Arabia and Dubai.
i Four or five hours.
j Twenty-four hours.

4 **What did they say?**

a Report what the general manager said.

'We are delighted to see how excited everyone is.'

He said they were …

b Report what the girl celebrating her birthday said.

'I love the Robot Restaurant.'

She said she …

c Report what Zoey the robot asked.

'Would you please make room for me?'

Zoey asked the customer …

Speaking

5 **Work in small groups. Discuss the following.**

a Why might built-in facial recognition be useful for robot waiters?
b Why does the restaurant also need human staff?
c What are the advantages and disadvantages of robots working as waiters?
d Apart from restaurants, in which other places could robots work?

Inside Bengaluru's
FIRST ROBOT RESTAURANT

Since the Robot Restaurant opened on 18 August, an average of 500 to 600 people have visited the restaurant every day. 'We are delighted to see how excited everyone is,' says Karthikeyan Ramesh, general manager of the restaurant.

The food at the restaurant is Indo-Asian. Each table has a digital tablet for selecting and ordering dishes. Once the food is prepared, a robot delivers it to the table. The restaurant was designed with extra space between the tables to help the robots move around easily.

Arya, Ramya, Zoey, Alice and Sansa may sound like characters from a fantasy series but in fact they are robot waiters, humanoids imported from China. They serve food while another robot acts as a receptionist, welcoming guests at the entrance of the restaurant. The manager explained that this receptionist robot registered customers' details when they visited for the first time. It has built-in facial recognition technology so it can greet customers by name when they return to the restaurant.

The manager also said that there were plans to open four or five more robot restaurants in India and two in the Middle East – one in Saudi Arabia and another one in Dubai.

The robots can interact with the customers. For example, they can sing 'Happy Birthday' for those celebrating their special day at the restaurant. A young customer said, 'I love the Robot Restaurant. It was a great surprise that a robot brought my birthday cake to the table. She even sang "Happy Birthday" for me as I cut the cake.'

The robots have to be charged for four or five hours. They can then work for 24 hours. The staff at the restaurant are trained to handle the robots in case of malfunction.

The robots themselves can deal with some problems. For instance, when a customer stood in the way as robot Zoey brought chocolate cake, Zoey stopped and said in a polite robotic voice, 'Excuse me, you are in my way. Would you please make room for me? Thank you.'

9.3 Time well spent?

In this lesson you will...

- ask and answer questions in a survey
- use pronouns such as *nobody*, *a few*.

- **How much time do you spend each day using a digital device?**

Listening

69

1 **Listen to Kyle and Zeena doing the survey on the opposite page. Note their answers.**

1 *K: c, d, f* *Z: …*

2 **Work with a partner. Listen again and check your answers.**

Use of English Indefinite and quantifying pronouns

all, everyone
almost all
a lot
quite a few
half
several
a few
not (that) many
very few, hardly anyone
nobody

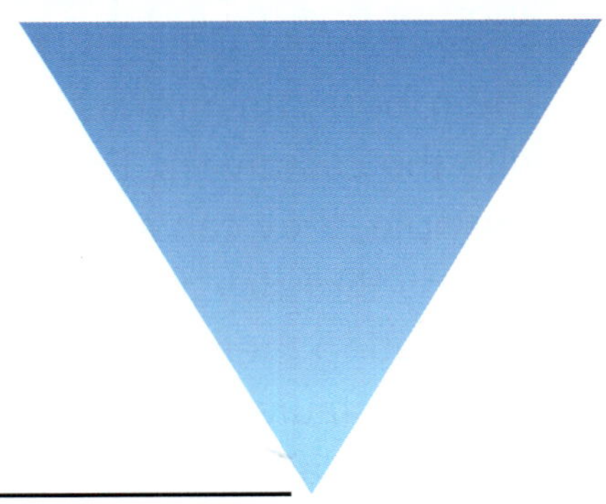

Language tip

Use *nobody*, *everyone and hardly anyone* with a singular verb: *Everyone has* a television.

Use all the other pronouns with a plural verb: *Not many have* an e-reader.

70

3 **Now listen to the survey results for Year 7, Kyle and Zeena's year group. Look at the expressions in the Use of English box. Which ones do you hear?**

Speaking

4 **Work in pairs. Talk about the results of the survey using the expressions in the Use of English box.**

A: *Nobody in Year 7 has got a desktop computer.*

B: *A lot have got a laptop.*

5 **Do the survey in your class. Report the results using the phrases in the Use of English box.**

6 Work in groups. Discuss these questions.

a Did anything in the survey results surprise you?

b Which do you think is the most useful digital device mentioned in the survey? Why?

c Are there any other digital devices that you think are really useful? What are they? Why are they useful?

Digital devices – a survey

1 Which of the following digital devices have you got?

- **a** A desktop computer
- **b** A laptop
- **c** A mobile (phone)
- **d** A tablet
- **e** An e-reader
- **f** A games console
- **g** A smartwatch
- **h** A television
- **i** Other (please specify)

2 Do you spend more time online and using digital devices than on other activities such as sport, music or reading (print books)?

Yes No

3 Do you think the time you spend using digital devices is always time well spent?

Yes No

4 Do you spend more time interacting with family and friends via digital devices than face to face?

Yes No

5 Do you think digital devices take up too much of your time?

Yes No

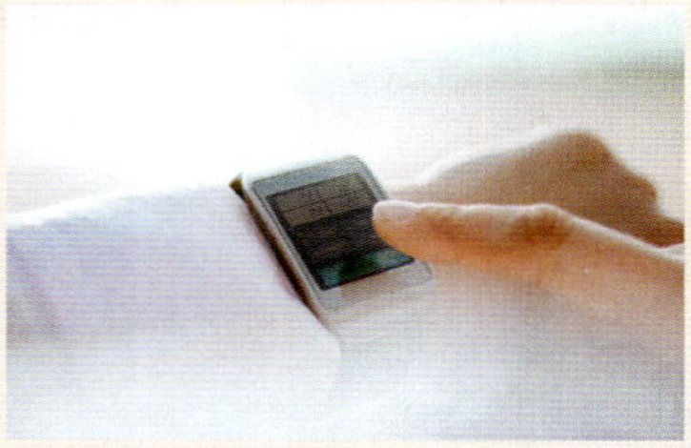

6 Do you feel anxious or uneasy without your phone, even for a short time?

Yes No

Year 7 – survey results

1 **a** 0% **b** 80% **c** 95% **d** 40% **e** 5% **f** 65% **g** 15% **h** 100%

2 Yes 60% No 40% **3** Yes 90% No 10%

4 Yes 10% No 90% **5** Yes 5% No 95%

6 Yes 75% No 25%

9.4 Zoom in!

In this lesson you will...

- give exact, detailed instructions in a logical order
- use multi-word verbs *switch on*, *hold down*, *type in*.

- **How good are you at giving detailed instructions? Explain to your partner exactly how to clean your teeth!**

  Open the tube of toothpaste. Pick up your toothbrush. Put …

Listening

71 **1** **You will hear a set of instructions. What are they for?**

2 **Work in pairs.**

Partner A: use the words in the first box to give the instructions to your partner.

switch on	application	web page
on/off button	search	zoom in
screen	internet	drop-down menu
password	icon	switch off
type in	key words	shut down
log in	website	
click on	window	

72 **3** **Now listen to the second set of instructions. What are they for?**

4 **Work in pairs.**

Partner B: use the words in the second box to give the instructions to your partner.

hold down	icon	key words
on/off button	touch	go
enter	application	scroll up/ down
passcode	internet	pinch
screen	type in	

Language tip

Remember that if you want to make instructions sound more polite, you can use the present simple.

You open the tube of toothpaste. You pick up your toothbrush.

Use of English **Multi-word verbs**

When you talk about digital technology, you often use a multi-word verb. This is a verb followed by a preposition / adverbial particle. For example, we **switch on** a computer or a mobile phone and we **type in** a password.

There can be more than one preposition / adverbial particle. For example, you can **zoom in on** the details.

Find six more verbs followed by prepositions / adverbial particles in the phrases in the vocabulary lists for Exercises 2 and 4.

5 **Complete each sentence with an appropriate verb followed by a preposition / adverbial particle.**

- a This is the airline's website address. You'll need to .... to the website and .... your password before you can confirm your flight.
- b It's hard to find the contact telephone number on this webpage, but if you .... the bottom of the page you'll find it there.
- c I think it's you in the background of the photo. .... that top corner and we'll be able to see.
- d Which symbol do I .... to reply to an email?
- e To get an accent over the e of café, ... the Alt key and press e. Then press e again.

Speaking

6 **Are you a computer whizz-kid? Explain to your partner, <u>in exact detail</u>, how to do the following:**

- a take a screenshot
- b take a selfie
- c add a name to your contacts list
- d forward a photo to a friend on your phone.
- e set an alarm on your phone
- f find out what the weather will be like tomorrow
- g use a tablet or smartphone to record a video
- h play a favourite song or piece of music using a music download app

9.5 Farming for the future

In this lesson you will...

- find out about technology in farming
- use clauses with *if* and *unless.*

- **Why do we need to find new ways of producing food?**

Reading

1 **Read about farming for the future. Which paragraphs do the photos illustrate?**

Farming for the **FUTURE**

Thirty metres below a London high street, there's an underground farm where salad crops are grown. They are harvested and delivered within an hour to local restaurants and supermarkets. Being underground means the temperature never goes below 15°C. More crops can be grown in a year than on a traditional outdoor farm. If you grow crops such as salad outside, you get up to three crops a year but if you grow them inside you can grow them all year round.

In Sweden there is a project to develop insect-breeding farms on nine roundabouts in Stockholm, the capital. Why? Because with the increasing urban population, scientists want to find a way of producing an alternative source of protein to meat.

In Rotterdam in the Netherlands, there is a floating dairy farm. Why? If global warming continues to cause sea levels to rise, the fields in low-lying coastal areas will be underwater. This means that unless we find an alternative, we won't be able to produce as many dairy products.

If you look very carefully at a cornfield in Hampshire in the south of England, you might see Tom, Dick or Harry. Who are they? They're robots that plant seeds and can even use a precision laser to kill weeds.

Vocabulary and speaking

Key words: Science and technology

laser
protein
seeds
temperature

2 **Work in pairs. Look at the words in the science and technology key words box and play a word association game. Who can think of the most words related to each one in the list?**

3 **Work in pairs. Each student chooses two paragraphs from the farming text. Read the paragraphs carefully, then tell your partner what you have read without looking at the text.**

Use of English *if* clauses

Zero conditional

Use the zero conditional to talk about things that are generally true.

present tense ... present tense

If you grow *crops such as salad outside,* ***you get*** *up to three crops a year.*

First conditional

Use the first conditional to talk about future situations that are real or possible.

present tense ... *will* future

If *global warming* ***continues****, the fields in low-lying coastal areas* ***will be*** *underwater.*

You can also use *unless* in conditional sentences.

First conditional with *unless*

Unless we find *an alternative,* ***we won't be able to*** *produce as many dairy products.*

If we don't find *an alternative,* ***we won't be able to*** *produce as many dairy products.*

Note that *unless* means *if … not.*

4 **Write out each sentence in your notebook using the correct option.**

a If we (*will want / want*) to produce food efficiently and sustainably, it's important to use technology to help us.
If we <u>want</u> to produce food …

b Unless we develop more urban farming, we (*aren't able / won't be able*) to reduce carbon emissions from transport.

c If you (*will grow / grow*) crops outside, you need sunlight and rain.

d If robots do all the jobs on farms in the future, fewer people (*are needed / will be needed*).

e We won't have enough food in the future, unless we (*act / will act*) now.

f People accept new technology if they (*understand / will understand*) the benefits.

5 **Look back at the text 'Farming for the future'. Discuss these questions using *if* and *unless*.**

a What are the advantages of the methods described?

b Are there any disadvantages?

9.6 Doing without digital

In this lesson you will...

- listen to someone talking about a challenge
- learn words and phrases that are useful in conversation.

- **A challenge is something that is difficult and that tests your ability or determination. Have you ever faced a challenge?**

Listening

73 **1** **You're going to hear Idris talking about a challenge that his school set him and his classmates. What was the challenge?**

2 **Listen again and choose the correct answers.**

1 **How long did the challenge last?**
   a two days
   b five days
   c one week

2 **Idris did two things during the challenge that he didn't usually do. What were they?**
   a He watched a video.
   b He watched a film on TV.
   c He read a book.

3 **Which two sports does Idris play?**
   a football
   b volleyball
   c basketball

4 **In which country does Idris have family?**
   a South Africa
   b Canada
   c Kenya

3 **Now answer these questions. Listen again if you need to.**

a What was Idris's view of the challenge at the beginning? How did his view change?
b What did Idris find difficult during the challenge? Mention three things.
c What did he learn from the challenge?

4 Listen again and complete the sentences.

- a I felt ……… lost.
- b I watched a ……… good film on TV.
- c I played football ……… after school.
- d I felt ……… relaxed.
- e I ……… picked up a book.
- f I didn't ……… think about using my phone.
- g It's ……… part of what I do.

5 Complete the sentences with an appropriate word or phrase from Exercise 4.

- a Unless I get eight hours sleep a night, I feel ……… tired in the morning.
- b It's not a good idea to go swimming ……… after lunch.
- c It's not impossible to survive a week without digital devices. It ……… feels very strange.
- d We all watch films on our laptops. We don't ……… have a television.
- e Are you ……… sure you didn't leave your phone at home?
- f I was ……… worried about going to a summer camp where phones were banned, but there was so much to do, I didn't miss having one.

6 Write sentences that are true for you using the words and phrases from Exercise 4.

I usually have a guitar lesson straight after school on a Wednesday.

I love cooking. I even make dinner for my parents sometimes.

Language tip

Look at the words and phrases you've used to complete the sentences in Exercise 4. You use them to make your conversation sound more natural. You can also use them when you're writing in an informal or conversational style.

9.7 Improve your writing

In this lesson you will...

- give a presentation about the advantages of using digital devices.

1 **A class was asked to prepare a presentation on 'The effect of screen time on young children'. Read the presentation on the opposite page.**

2 **Now read the notes on the structure of the presentation. Then answer the questions.**

a Does the title give a clear idea of what the presentation is about?
b How does the opening statement capture the audience's attention?
c What key information does the student give?
d Which examples does the student give?
e What data does the student give?
f How does the student end the presentation?

3 **Look at the first four slides on the opposite page that the student prepared for the presentation. Prepare two more slides for the last two paragraphs.**

4 **You are going to prepare a presentation on 'The advantages of using digital devices' for people of your age.**

Step 1: Plan what you're going to say.
Step 2: Do some research to find information and data to support your argument.
Step 3: Write your presentation using the one on the opposite page as a model.
Step 4: Make your slides using the ones on the opposite page as a model.
Step 5: Ask another student to check your presentation and slides.
Step 6: Make any changes that are needed.
Step 7: Give your presentation.

- Does your title give a clear idea of what your presentation is about?
- Does the opening statement capture the audience's attention?
- Have you given examples to support the key information?
- Have you included data to support your argument?
- Did you end your presentation with a conclusion?

- watching TV
- playing computer games
- looking at screens on phones and tablets

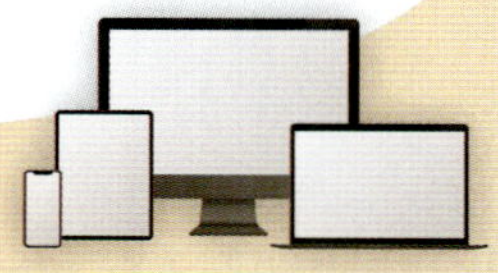

- 2400 children, aged 2–3, Canada
- language and problem-solving skills
- physical coordination

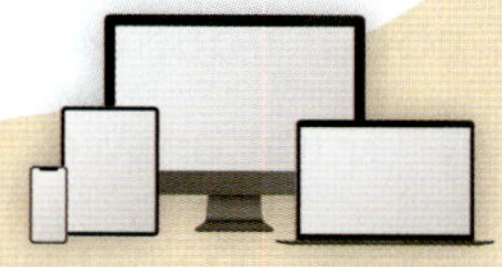

- worse test results at 3 and 5

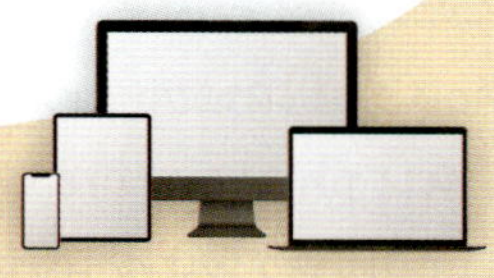

- ✗ physical activities
- ✗ talking to people
- ✗ interacting with people

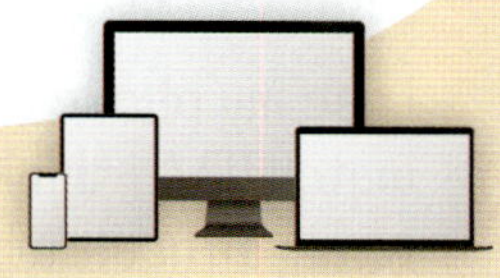

The effect of screen time on young children

It's bad for young children to spend too much time watching TV, playing computer games or looking at screens on phones and tablets.

This is the conclusion of a survey of 2400 children in Canada. The amount of time two- and three-year-olds spend in front of a screen has a negative effect on their language and problem-solving skills, as well as their physical coordination.

Children who spent a lot of time in front of a screen at the ages of two and three had worse test results at three and five than other children.

If children are looking at screens, they're not doing physical activities. They're also missing opportunities to talk and interact with people.

The study found that children watched screens for an average of 17.09 hours per week at age two, 24.99 hours at age three, and 10.85 hours at age five.

The researchers have asked doctors and other health workers to encourage families to limit the amount of time children spend in front of a screen. They suggest having 'screen-free' zones and 'device curfews' in the home.

Choose a title that gives a clear idea of what your presentation is about.

Capture your audience's attention with a bold statement.

Support the statement with key information.

Give examples to support your argument.

Support your argument with data.

Give a conclusion / say what can be done.

9.8 Project challenge

Project 1: Digital challenge

You're going to try do without digital devices for a time. Then you're going to write about your experience.

1 First answer these questions.

a Which digital devices do you use? (Phone, laptop, TV, tablet, other.) Make a list.

b What do you think is going to be the most difficult to give up? Why?

c When are you going to start your challenge? Give an exact time.

2 Keep a diary of your digital challenge. Look at the models to help you. Remember that you will have to write by hand!

Monday 17.00

I use my phone a lot and I often watch TV. I think it's going to be really difficult without my phone, but I think I can survive until this time tomorrow evening.

Monday 19.00

Oh no, I can't remember what my English homework is and I can't ask my friend to send it to me because I can't use my phone! And if I don't do my homework I'll be in trouble. I need to send my friend a text to ask him.

Monday 19.30

My digital challenge lasted two hours!

Monday 17.00

I use my phone, a laptop and I also use a tablet at home. I use my phone more than the other two things, but I think I can do without them until tomorrow.

Monday 21.00

I've finished my homework, but it seems a bit strange that I can't check my messages or use my laptop. I think I'll read my book.

Tuesday 13.00 (lunchtime)

I wanted to text my friend to ask her to meet me on the way home, but I didn't and that was OK.

Tuesday 18.00

I've done it! I managed to do without digital devices for 24 hours. It was quite easy and I had more time to do other things. It made me feel quite relaxed.

3 Compare your diaries. Who found the challenge quite easy? Who found it really hard? Who lasted the longest?

- How did the model diary help you to write your own diary?
- What did you learn from your classmates' diaries?

Project 2: A debate

You are going to have a class debate about the following topic: 'Digital devices have more advantages than disadvantages'.

Step 1: Divide the class into two groups: those who agree with the statement above and those who disagree with it.

Step 2: Follow these steps.

- Choose someone to lead your group.
- Look back at the lessons in this unit to give you ideas.
- Share your ideas and opinions in a brainstorming session.
- Remember that you need facts and examples to support your argument.
- Your leader will make a note of your ideas and opinions. Everyone has to say something in the debate. The leader will decide on the order.

Step 3: Have your debate. Remember to listen respectfully to other people's opinions.

Don't talk or interrupt when someone else is speaking.

Try to use these phrases in your debate.

Speaking tip

Make a note of phrases you use in the discussion and learn them.

Expressing opinions	Agreeing	Disagreeing
I think (that) …	I agree …	I see your point, but …
I believe (that) …	That's right.	But don't you think …?
It seems to me (that) …	Exactly.	I don't agree …
I'm in favour of … (followed by verb + *-ing*)	Absolutely!	I don't agree at all …
I'm against … (followed by verb + *-ing*)		

- What did you learn from doing this project?
- What did you find easy?
- What did you find difficult?

9.9 Non-fiction

***A Little History of the World* by E.H. Gombrich**

Ernst Gombrich was an art historian and teacher. He said that *A Little History of the World* wasn't intended to be like a school history textbook: 'I would like my readers to relax, and to follow the story without having to take notes or to memorise names and dates.'

74

1 Read about Ernst Gombrich. Then read and listen to the extract from *A Little History of the World*. What is the topic of the extract?

2 Read the extract again and answer the questions.

a Ernst Gombrich mentions two important contributions to world knowledge from Arabic culture. What are they?

b What are the two number systems mentioned in the text?

c According to Gombrich, which number system is easier to work with, and why?

d Which of the two contributions to world knowledge does the writer think has been more important?

3 The author uses the following techniques. Find examples of them in the text.

a asking the reader questions

b addressing the reader directly

c using adjectives which show his opinion

d making comparisons

e an informal conversational style.

There are two things for which I am especially grateful to the Arabs. First, the wonderful tales they used to tell and then wrote down, which you can read in *One Thousand and One Nights*. The second is even more fabulous than the tales, although you may not think so. Listen! Here is a number: '12'. Now why do you think we say 'twelve' rather than 'one-two' or 'one and two'? 'Because,' you say, 'the one isn't really a one at all, but a ten.' Do you know how the Romans wrote '12'? Like this: 'XII'. And 112? 'CXII'. And 1112? 'MCXII'. Just think of trying to multiply and add up with Roman numbers like these! Whereas with our 'Arabic' numbers it's easy. Not just because they're attractive and easy to write, but because they contain something new: place value – the value given to a number on account of its position. A number placed on the left of two others has to be a hundred number. So we write one hundred with a one followed by two zeros.

Could you have come up with such a useful invention? I certainly couldn't. We owe it to the Arabs, who themselves owe it to the Indians. And in my opinion that invention is even more amazing than all the Thousand and One Nights put together.

Did you know?

There are seven symbols from which all Roman numbers are made:

I	1	C	100
V	5	D	500
X	10	M	1000
L	50		

There is no equivalent of 0.

Look at the numbers 1 to 12 on the clock face using Roman numerals. Explain how the Romans made the numbers 6, 7, 8, 11 and 12. Then explain how they made the numbers 4 and 9.

75

4 Read and listen to the second extract. It is from a book called *A History of the World in 100 Objects* by Neil MacGregor. What does it describe?

5 Look up any words you don't know in a dictionary.

A History of the World in 100 Objects was originally a series of radio programmes. The listeners could not see the objects described; they had to imagine them.

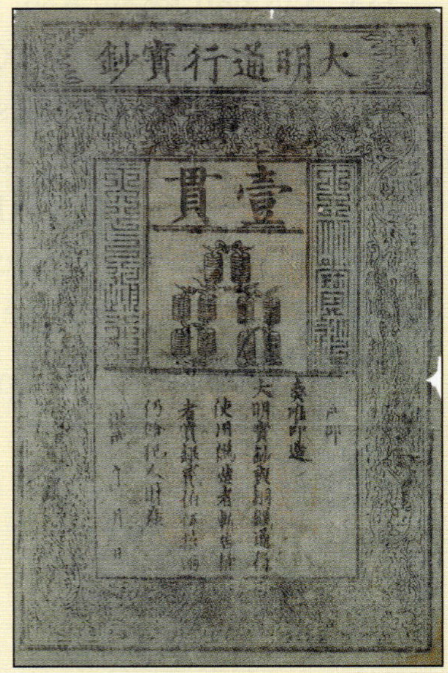

At first glance, this note doesn't look at all like modern paper money. It is paper, obviously enough, and it's larger than a sheet of A4. It's a soft, velvety grey colour, and it's made out of mulberry bark, which was the legally approved material for Chinese paper money at the time. The fibres of mulberry bark are long and flexible, so even today, though it's around 600 years old, the paper is still soft and pliable.

It is fully printed on only one side, a woodblock stamp in black ink with Chinese characters and decorative features arranged in a series of rows and columns. Along the top, six bold characters announce that this is the 'Great Ming Circulating Treasure Certificate'. Below this there is a decorative border of dragons all round the sheet – dragons of course being one of the traditional symbols of China and of its emperor. Just inside the border are two columns of text, the one on the left announcing again that this is the 'Great Ming Circulating Treasure Certificate' and the one on the right saying that this is 'To Circulate For Ever'.

That's quite a claim. How permanent can for ever be? In stamping the promise on to the very note, the Ming state seems to be asserting that it too will be around for ever to honour it.

6 Answer these questions.

- a How did Neil MacGregor make the object seem real to the people listening to the radio programme?
- b What details does he focus on? The age? The colour? …

7 Notice how he uses *even*, *just* and *quite* to make the style more conversational. What else can you say about the style of the writing? Is it formal, informal or somewhere between the two?

8 Write a description of a bank note from your country. Use the text above as a model.

Check your progress

General knowledge quiz

How much can you remember about what you have learned?

1 What do you find in a 'contacts list'?

2 What is an e-reader?

3 Applications are used in many digital devices. What are they generally known as?

4 If a computer or robot 'malfunctions', what happens?

5 If robots have built-in facial recognition technology, what can they do?

6 What is a 'dairy farm'? Why is there a floating dairy farm in Rotterdam?

7 What is the capital of Sweden?

8 Scientists believe that sea levels are rising due to .... warming.

9 What kind of products are milk, yoghurt, butter and cheese?

10 What do insects contain that makes them a possible alternative to meat?

Vocabulary

Digital devices

1 **Match the words with the pictures.**

download	emoji
upload	Wi-Fi

2 **Complete the words.**

a You press the on / off b .... n to switch your computer on.

b If the s .... n is too bright or too dark, you can change it by pressing:

c You click on the icon for the a .... n you want.

d Click on the red button to close the w .... w.

e To log in, type your p .... d.

3 **Choose the correct option.**

a When you're travelling, you don't have to print *out / down* your boarding pass.

b Type *in / off* your password.

c You'll find the details you need if you scroll *in / down* to the bottom.

d Zoom *in on / down on* see it clearly.

e To get more information, click *to / on* the link at the top of the page.

f To get the euro symbol, hold *down / on* the Alt key and press '2'.

g Remember to switch *off / out* your computer at the end of the day.

Use of English

1 Report these statements, questions and requests.

a David: I write my blog every day.

David said he wrote his blog every day.

b Alisha: I need a new laptop.

c Maya: Do you use the calculator on your phone, Sara?

Maya asked Sara if she used the calculator on her phone.

d Benedict: Do you do your homework on your laptop, Lee?

e Diego: José, please show me how to turn your phone off.

Diego asked José how to turn his phone off.

f Nicole: Take a photo of us, Lauren.

2 Rewrite the sentences using *unless*.

a If you don't get enough sleep, you'll feel tired all day.

Unless you get enough sleep, you'll feel tired all day.

b If you don't charge your phone now, you won't be able to call me later.

c If I don't write things down, I don't remember them.

d I often forget to reply to texts if I don't respond to them straight away.

3 Complete the sentences with the correct verb forms.

a	If I ***have*** time, I***'ll phone*** you later.	*have*	*phone*
b	I .... you the link if you .... me your email address.	*send*	*give*
c	If you .... your laptop round, we .... our homework together.	*bring*	*do*
d	If you .... a new phone, you .... a new charger.	*get*	*need*
e	Unless there .... Wi-Fi at the campsite, we .... watch a film.	*be*	*not be able to*

Summary checklist

I can

- ☐ read and discuss an article about a robot restaurant.
- ☐ answer questions in a survey about digital devices and discuss how useful they are.
- ☐ understand and give instructions for using a computer and a mobile phone.
- ☐ discuss recent and future developments in farming.
- ☐ give a presentation about digital devices.
- ☐ write diary entries describing a digital challenge.
- ☐ take part in a debate.